SKYROCKET
YOUR CAREER

*The No Bullsh*t Approach to Find Your Dream Job, Be Successful in It, and Transform into a Rockstar.*

RAJ SUBRAMEYER

ChaiLatte Press
2020

Library of Congress Control Number : 2020914069

Published by ChaiLatte Press

Ordering Information:

Quantity sales: Special discounts are available on quantity purchases by corporations, associations, and others. For details, contact the publisher at the e-mail address above.

Printed in the United States of America

ISBN 978-1-73515-620-0 (paperback)
ISBN 978-1-73515-621-7 (ebook)
www.skyrocketyourcareerbook.com

This book is dedicated to my wife, Carlene, and my son Neil. They continue to inspire me and make me a better man, parent, and friend every day.

CONTENTS

Foreword

As I write this, the world is experiencing a bunch of new normals. We are in a global pandemic. Social justice reforms are in full swing and unemployment is high. Really high. To put it bluntly, there is a lot of uncertainty and with uncertainty comes instability and insecurity. During times like these, we look for guides to help us identify problems and obstacles. That's where Raj comes in. His story is an example of what one can do when normalcy seems like a foreign concept.

Before I dive into why Raj is a great guide though, I want to talk about my connection to Raj and the topic of this book. I met Raj through my best friend and much like with kindred spirits, we connected over shared passions as well as shared obstacles. Like Raj, I have spent most of my life being the odd one out. Like Raj, I am an immigrant, and like Raj, I was expected to be a lawyer, engineer, or doctor after I graduated from college. Any other option would have been considered a failure. At least by my loved ones and peers and when you come from a collectivist background where the family is a big deal, your career choice is a BIG DEAL because it is seen as an indicator of success.

Success, though, isn't something many of us truly own. Many of us buy into a version of success that has nothing to do with our true desires. Essentially, we choose to become strangers to ourselves so that we can be accepted by the society that often rejects our individuality. These rejections come at a price that many of us consider too steep to pay. Ostracization, isolation, and shame. A lot of us continue this cycle when we have kids of our own because we want to spare our kids from the same pain we worked so hard to avoid.

I can't explain it but for some reason, I decided to find out what success looks like outside of what was expected of me. I wanted to go on a different journey from my peers when I was younger and what a road it has been. It led me to 85 plus job rejections, being fired twice, and being broke multiple times in one of the most expensive cities in the world. However, with every story comes perspective and multiple points of view. The perspective I gained was that on the other side of ostracization, isolation, and shame is the discovery of self. And this, I found to be more priceless than what I was taught to avoid most of my life. That navigation from other people's expectations of myself to my expectation of myself led me to the career I have now as a bestselling author, speaker, consultant, and professor.

All of this is to say that when I read Raj's book, I found myself tremendously grateful because of the genuine heartfelt nature of his writing style as well as how structured he was with his pieces of advice. Rarely do you find books that are both compassionate and authentic, and *Skyrocket Your Career* is such a book. Raj says in the book that "to become a legend, you need to start doing legendary work," and I couldn't agree more. A lot of this "legendary" comes from a deep knowledge of self and willingness to be yourself. The good thing is that with this book, you're not just getting platitudes, you're getting a roadmap to living your best life.

Cheers to finding comfort in new normals!

Yours truly,
Tayo Rockson
Author of *Use Your Difference To Make A Difference* and CEO of UYD Management

Introduction

My Story

I grew up in the southern part of India in a conservative upper middle-class family. My father grew up poor, and he worked hard to support not only us but his parents and siblings as well. Since he was a kid, he excelled in academics and studied his entire life on scholarships. Needless to say, my elder brother and I were strongly encouraged to focus on academics. My mom was an English teacher, and after their marriage, she took on the critical role of a homemaker, bringing my brother and me up. I am the younger one of the two kids.

I am grateful that my parents did everything they could to give my brother and me the best possible life and education. I still practice the principles that my dad instilled in me—hard work, dedication, generosity, and the courage to handle any obstacles that come my way.

When I was growing up in Chennai, kids were molded to focus on three kinds of careers—Doctor, Engineer, or Lawyer. Back in the 1980's, these were the highest-paying jobs, and people in these professions were greatly respected in society. In addition, work had a different meaning—it was about earning money, buying a house, purchasing a car, settling down, getting married, and having kids. Naturally, kids were encouraged to focus on jobs with the highest return on investment (ROI). Also, in India, ROI is everything. It is all about trying to get as many gains as possible for the effort you put in. This is reflected in all aspects of life: bargaining with vendors at street markets, buying a car and expecting it to survive for 100 years without any mainte-nance, making sure you marry into a family who is either more well-off than yours or highly esteemed in society, and the list goes on. This is also the reason why we can survive anywhere and adapt to most situations as we are always looking for opportunities and a chance to lead a better life.

Here I was, part of a family with a super-smart Dad and a genius brother, so the expectations from me to perform well in academics were really high. I was constantly compared to the overachievers around me and was under pressure to emulate them. This also led to a constant feeling within me that I was dumb, I was not good enough, I did not matter, and I was never going to be successful in life. I was the average Joe (well, in India, the average "Raj" since that's one of the most common names), and focusing on academics was not really my thing. I had other interests and passions, such as playing outdoor sports, hanging out with friends, and asking questions about things I did not understand (I was never really into indoor games, including video games; yes, I am a rare exception for being a nerd). Also, where I come from in southern India, it is not popular or accepted to ask questions. You need to follow things as they are because of pressure from family, culture, and society. You get reprimanded if you challenge the status quo.

All this constant comparison to the high performers around me, and getting rebuked for asking questions, made me feel like an outcast. I developed social anxiety, fear of rejection, and shut myself out from other people. Outside, I was acting as if everything was normal, but inside, I was engulfed with frustration, anger, sadness, and confusion about my life and identity. I was going through low self-esteem, high self-doubt, and severe body image issues. I used food as a coping mechanism for social pressures and was ridiculed for my weight and appearance throughout my life.

The Awakening

The trigger event happened during the second year of my undergraduate course. I still remember this vividly; I was in my room and reflecting on my life. My chest was pounding as if I was getting a heart attack. I was tired of living within a shell, and my body and mind were struggling to break free. Then it happened—20 years of living a life with a false identity, killing myself internally to please others around me, yearning for validation from others that I was good enough, not being able to be myself and do things which I felt were right for me—all these feelings that had bottled up within me exploded. I cried for two hours straight, wondering what I needed to do next. I wanted to do something that would give me a purpose and meaning in life, and I aspired to find my true passion and identity. This was when I decided that I am good enough, I matter, I can strive for greatness, and I can carve my own identity. I declared power over my life.

There were two things I wanted to change about myself: (1) get rid of my anxiety and fear of rejection when speaking to people and (2) pursue my true passion and career path (after finding out what it was, of course). To tackle my first obstacle, I started participating in cultural events, making new friends, and inserting myself into awkward conversations with family and friends. This forced me to get out of my comfort zone. Also, I started doing part-time jobs to meet new people, learn life skills, and interact with people. I took this new mindset with me throughout the rest of my undergraduate years and entered the corporate environment in 2006. In the next four years, I worked my butt off to learn everything I could and said yes to every opportunity that came my way. I kept an open mind and found mentors and coaches to help me grow and discover my passion. This was when I realized that I love collaborating with people and finding solutions to help others.

In 2011, I spent $3,000 of my own money to go to a software conference. Everyone thought I was crazy because here is the thing: in the software world, no one spends their own freaking money to go to a conference. Either the company you work for pays for it, or you go to the conference as a speaker, in which case the registration fee is waived (which is the bulk of the expense). But I wanted a change in my boring life and also wanted to learn something new. So, I took a leap of faith and decided to invest in myself. At the conference, I saw many people speak and share their experiences with the audience on various topics. Some sessions were good, and some were bad. I should say it is good to have sessions with bad content and/or delivery, as it gives people confidence that anyone can give a conference talk. At least in my life, this made a difference, since that is when I decided that I should give a talk to get rid of my fear of public speaking. I spoke with many speakers at the conference, took a lot of notes, and went back home feeling inspired.

To become a legend, you need to start doing legendary work. This is what separates the majority of people who want to become legends from those who actually become them. Most of us have ambitions, dreams, goals; we feel inspired after attending motivational events, hearing success stories, and seeing entrepreneurs start million-dollar businesses. The problem comes a couple of days later—the procrastination starts, then life happens, and the motivating event is already forgotten. How many of us have been in this situation before? I, for one, was always a person who did not take any action. But for once, I decided that after coming back from the conference, I needed to keep the momentum going.

After the conference, I read books and watched videos on public speaking. I videotaped myself speaking, and asked my then-girlfriend-now-wife, a collegiate public-speaking champion, to critique my video and speaking style (I should say this was one of the few occasions she took advantage of, and she gave me a feeling that I was a contestant in American Idol, berated by Simon Cowell). In 2012, I started speaking at small meetup groups and events. Then in 2013, after 7 months and 23 trial runs with various groups of people to get feedback, I finally gave my first conference talk. Mine was one of the best sessions at the conference, and the rest is history. That one decision to invest in myself made me who I am today—an international keynote speaker, inspiring people globally. This experience made me realize that a mindset shift and consistency are keys to succeed in anything and also helped me discover my true passion and career path, which is inspiring people through my stories and experiences.

It also made me realize that anything is possible if you put in the effort, stay focused and motivated, and have explicit goals. I have since applied these principles to my career as well.

Career Growth

During that second year of undergrad, when I had the trigger event which propelled me to change my life, I was also endlessly getting pressure from family and friends to follow a particular career path they thought was right for me. For the first 20 years of my life, I lived by other people's rules and let other people control my life and make decisions for me. I was wearing a false identity, which society had thrown upon me. I was tired of this bullshit and decided to take matters in my own hands. The first step involved my higher education (or lack thereof).

Despite being pressured to pursue my master's program in the United States immediately after I graduate, I decided to figure out what I wanted to do in life by staying in Chennai and working there. My career path was going to be my choice.

During the campus recruitment season in undergrad, numerous companies come to recruit graduates. In my final year, I think I attended about 22 interviews, and in most of them, I made the final round but got rejected, as I got nervous about getting the job (and it showed through in the interviews). After that many interviews, my mind was numb, and for the next one, I said, *Fuck it, I am just going to attend the interview and see what happens.*

Apparently, this kind of attitude of "I do not give a shit" works sometimes. I went to the final round of interviews, and that company finally decided to give me a job at a minimal salary. After this experience, I decided to take this attitude with me wherever I go till this day.

I took up a job in a field called software testing. It was a new, "hot" field back then but did not pay much. I had no idea what the job was about but knew it was in the IT space, which was the field I wanted to get into. As expected, I was ridiculed for having an unheard-of job by a lot of people. I continued to adopt the "I do not give a shit" attitude, which helped me ignore the noise around me.

Since there weren't that many successful software testers at my company at that time, I took it as an opportunity to excel at my job. I was open to every opportunity that came my way and even volunteered to do shitty jobs just to get introduced to more people in the company. All this effort paid off when I was rated a star performer in many of the following years that I worked at that first company. This role also helped me figure out my specialization for my master's program, and eventually led to my relocation to the United States in 2008 to pursue my Master's in Software Engineering.

Since then, I have sought out different opportunities that came my way and kept an open mind. I found mentors and coaches who were able to help me. I started as a software tester, moved into software development, began leading teams, became a developer evangelist, and eventually transitioned into becoming an entrepreneur, along the way leading numerous people to transform their careers to make an impact on themselves and others.

Why Is Your Career Important?

How often have you heard employers and employees say they value work-life balance? The answer is always. I am going to break it to you—such a thing as work-life balance does not exist unless you stop working, move to some exotic place like the Maldives or another beach destination, and live your life without having to think about money. By then, you would consider "work" as getting out of bed and spending all day on the beach, of course drinking some tropical cocktails during your all-day happy hour. As long as you have ambitions, the entrepreneurial itch, or the urge to make an impact in other people's lives through your actions, you are going to continue to work while having a personal life. The amount of time you work may vary, but you will still have to manage both, and sometimes, one takes over the other. There is never a perfect balance if you are working right. As Richard Branson says, *Work is not separate from play and play is not separate from work, it's all living.*

Research suggests[1] that one-third of your life is spent at work. On average, a person will spend 90,000 hours at work over a lifetime. Holy fuck! That is a lot of time away from family. Of course, this is just the average; with all of the advancements in technology, people are working longer hours in various industries. For many, work has become the new family, which is sad but true.

So the career you choose is significant, and a lot of effort needs to go into finding your dream job. What is a "dream job?" I define it as a job that will help you wake up every morning feeling excited, that makes you happy, and that has an impact on your and other people's lives.

Obstacles to Finding Your Dream Job

The human mind is funny. One day it tells you that you are the best person in this world, and the very next day, it is going to tell you that you are a loser. It is as if it is always high on pot; it is so random. But, what if I said you can control your mind and make it listen to you? The transformation starts with YOU.

---

[1] "One third of your life is spent at work—Gettysburg College." https://www.gettysburg.edu/news/stories?id=79db7b34-630c-4f49-ad32-4ab9ea48e72b&pageTitle=1%2F3+of+your+life+is+spent+at+work.

We are so worried about other people's opinions and often fear the unknown. We make so many assumptions about what will happen if we make a change. A whole story about your future life is already written in your head before it even happens. Most of the narratives do not pan out in real life, since circumstances take us in a totally different direction. Then, why do we dream up these narratives in the first place? Why can't we train our minds to imagine a positive story instead of a negative one? Yes, positive change is possible, and I will show you how.

The biggest obstacles holding people down based on my experiences are immigration status, fear, and a lack of any combination of confidence, time, clarity, and motivation. Not many people think that the immigration status would be an obstacle because for many of them, it's not. I am an immigrant and came to the United States on a student visa. It was fucking hell for me to get a job; I arrived in America on August 31st, 2008, and the recession started the week after. Upon finishing my graduate degree in 2010, most companies were not willing to sponsor my work visa, which is needed to work in the United States legally (more on this in Chapter 1). Your immigration status may limit the opportunities you have and could make it more challenging for you to get your dream job. This does not mean it is impossible to get hired, but it often takes more effort than if you don't need to worry about it. So the next time you meet an immigrant, have some sympathy for them, as they have to go through a lot of shit just to be qualified for many positions.

Another reason why people do not want to make a change is that they get comfortable in their current job (which they actually hate) and keep convincing themselves that it is a good thing they still have a job. They assume this gives them stability in life. They feel they need to support and take care of their family and do not want to make a change that may risk anything. As happened in my early adult life in India, they don't want society to judge them for their career choices.

If there is one thing we have learned from the global COVID-19 pandemic or the 2008 recession, it is that there is nothing stable in life. A person working their ass off for 30 years gets laid off, along with a person who has been working in the company only for a year. Companies do not give a fuck when it comes to laying off people. They need to cover their ass first and do what is best for the company. So, unfortunately, certain people and departments come under the chopping block. This is reality. In life, there is only opportunity, not stability. If this is the case, then why not take a chance by making a change and do something meaningful in life?

Let me fill you in on a secret: you are more badass than you think you are. I know this because I went through the same emotions of fear, anxiety, lack of confidence, and low self-esteem. Then I decided that I was going to take control of my destiny and not let circumstances control it.

Remember, *you cannot change the circumstances, but you can control your actions in any circumstance and make a positive change.*

How Will This Book Change Your Life?

It took me over 15 years to realize that I had everything it took to be a rockstar. I consumed hundreds of books, podcasts, articles, and blog posts. I interviewed various leaders in the industry and studied under them as an apprentice. I worked for great managers led high-performing teams myself. After innumerable failures and successes, I identified different strategies that transformed my life. The strategies and real-life experiences I share in this book have been tried and tested not only in my life but with numerous other successful people, who are currently leaders in their industry. My goal is to share all the tips, tricks, and tools in a structured way for you to get your dream job.

This book is divided into six chapters. In chapter 1, I discuss how to discover and find your dream job. It includes the introduction of the Discover, Plan, and Action (DPA) approach; identifying goals; and developing a plan to accomplish those goals. I share different actionable techniques and approaches that will help you find your dream job. In chapter 2, I discuss different strategies to prepare for the interview and ace it. Finally, we focus on getting you the money you deserve for the job by discussing different salary negotiation tricks. In chapter 3, I arm you with the tools to be successful in your career and ensure you earn great performance reviews. In chapter 4, I help you forge your own path, to set yourself miles apart from your competition. I reveal the techniques that made me a rockstar in my career. If an average guy like me can do it, so can you—I am going to show you how. In chapter 5, I examine strategies and tips to unleash your power for exponential growth. Each of these chapters contains exercises for you to practice these techniques and approaches that are going to transform your life. Finally, in chapter 6, I share my final thoughts on how you can take my message in this book and use it to make a positive impact on your life.

You are open to skip to any section that directly applies to your current situation; however, the recommended approach is to go through each part in order since each part builds upon the previous ones. Once you become a rockstar in one job, you are on your way to finding your next one.

The examples used in this book would tend to lean toward technical jobs because, well, what do you know—I am a tech career coach. But the strategies I describe in this book apply to ALL jobs. So, even if you don't work or want to transition into the IT space, there is still plenty of guidance for you.

My goal for my book is to be a guide to help you make good career choices, get you out of your comfort zone, and motivate you to make a positive change. Life is short, and it is time we did something meaningful with purpose. Let's get started…

We all have two lives, the second one starts when we realize we have only one

—Confucius

CHAPTER 1
Discovering Your Dream Job

. . . .

Tough times don't last, tough people do.
—Robert Schuller

Luck Favors the Brave

Picture it: August 31, 2008. I land at JFK airport in New York City. I get out of the gate, and a guy passes me and asks, "How is it going?" I reply saying, "I am doing good. I just landed from India…" But before I could continue, he continued on his way without acknowledging me. I keep walking toward the baggage claim, and another woman passes me and says, "How is it going?" This time I say, "I am good; I just landed from India…" And once again, this woman keeps going on without saying a word or acknowledging me. Finally, I get out of the airport, and another woman, about 30 years of age, passes me and says, "How is it going?" This time, I really wanted to let her know how it really was going (since I'd already started twice and been ignored). So, I started, "I am doing good. My name is Raj. I just landed. I came here to do my master's…" And kept walking with her while talking. Then, she turned to me with a frown on her face and said, "Weirdo." That was my first experience in the United States. Only later did I discover that no one gives a shit about you when they ask "How is it going?" in the United States. Apparently, it is a cultural thing, and many people use that phrase just to acknowledge your existence and as a quick greeting. Yup, it was a culture shock to me. I had many similar experiences throughout my life in the USA, but those I'll save for another book.

Finally, I reached Rochester, New York, where I was accepted to start my master's program in software engineering. I was super pumped and ready to go. Then on September 9, 2008, Lehman Brothers—one of the largest financial firms—had its shares plunge by 45 percent, and in a couple of days, they filed for bankruptcy. This was the largest bankruptcy filing in US history, as the company held about $600 billion in assets. The incident officially marked the start of the 2008 recession, and companies quickly followed in its footsteps. I had come to the United States with big dreams, and within a week, those dreams were crushed with the recession. Getting jobs was going to prove to be really hard, especially for non-US citizens who did not have work permits, like me. I came to the USA on a student visa, and I would need a company to sponsor my work permit to legally work in the USA. Unfortunately, none of the companies had the money or time to sponsor work permits, and even US citizens were finding it hard to get jobs.

I had come to study first, then work. So I decided to continue my master's program and figure things out as the days passed by (or, using a new-to-me American idiom, *I'd cross that bridge when I got there*). In 2009, I started wondering what would my life look like after I graduated? If I wanted to stay in the United States, I had to figure out a way to get a job at a company willing to sponsor my work visa. Was this just a far-fetched dream? Or did I have what it takes to ride the wave? All these thoughts were going through my mind; meanwhile, I was still taking my courses and trying to ace them.

By mid-2009, half of my class, who were international students, decided to head back home after graduation. It all came down to two choices: (1) go home and find a job in my native country or (2) do whatever it takes to try to get a job and stay in the United States. I chose the second option.

I started applying for work in large numbers. When I say "large numbers," I mean I applied to 1,293 positions from mid-2009 until the beginning of 2010. Guess how many callbacks I received after applying for that many jobs? The correct answer is FOUR: 0.3 percent! Yes, I said that right; I got callbacks from four companies who were willing to talk to me. Out of those four calls, guess how many I converted? I got ONE job offer, and it was an internship, NOT a full-time position. During that time, you could do an internship on a student visa and extend your stay in the US for the duration of the internship. Since I could not think of any other option to continue my stay, I took up the internship. Then I worked my ass off and attended different campus recruitment events in parallel. Finally, another company was interested in my experience; one thing led to another, and I landed a full-time job after six months at the internship.

That one decision I made of riding the wave and doing whatever it took to get a job finally paid off, and it significantly changed my life. Fast-forward to where I am now; I am an international keynote speaker, writer, and tech career coach and have built a six-figure business. I have impacted so many people's personal lives and careers through my experiences and helped them build a better future for themselves and others. All these things would not have happened without that one decision I made in 2009. There is a saying *Fortune favors the bold* by Virgil; you may not be able to control the circumstances around you, but fear and scarcity can help you find opportunities that you may otherwise not discover if you are living a cushy and comfortable life.

So what was my strategy to finally land a job? I applied for 1,293 jobs, and for the first 500 I applied for, I did not have any clue what I was doing. Quite frankly, I was naive. I did not have a strategy, did not know what kind of job I wanted, and did not know what my end goal was. After 15 years of working in various industries and roles, and helping numerous people get their dream job (including myself), I started figuring out common patterns which helped to identify ideal career paths and land dream jobs. From these patterns, I identified eight strategies that have helped my coaching clients become rockstar leaders in their industries, like vice presidents, CTOs, and directors.

One of my first experiences of sharing these strategies was with my wife, shortly after we started dating. She has a bachelor's in history and minors in political science and European studies. These strategies helped her transition from a call center representative in 2011 to a software tester, and finally, to a senior IT developer and analyst working on high-profile government projects.

Ready to find that dream job? The nine strategies described in the upcoming sections will show you how.

The DPA Approach

Everything you do is a strategy; you focus on accomplishing a goal to bring you closer to your vision. The problem for the majority of the people is that they do not know what they want. Without knowing what you want, how do you know what to focus on?

This is where the DPA approach helps to give you focus and an actionable plan for career growth. I have used this approach in my life, and all of my clients have used it to get them closer to their dream job and set them up for success. This is the first thing you need to do before starting anything related to your career—you can't know what direction to go in if you don't know what your destination is.

The DPA approach has three stages: Discovery, Plan, and Action.

Stage 1: D—DISCOVERY

This stage is all about identifying your strengths and discovering patterns from those strengths.

There are two steps under this stage:

Step 1: *Find your interests*
- Mind Dump Exercise

More information about this is later in the chapter. This is an exercise to identify the things you like and hate to do.

- Identifying success stories throughout your career

Write down all the success stories you can think of in your current and previous jobs. Specifically, focus on:

- What did you do?
- What impact did you make?
- How did it make you feel?

- Identify what you would be proud to do that you can do for others?

Write down all the things that would make an impact on other people's lives and make them feel proud of you and your work.

Step 2: *Identify your buckets*
Based on all the information you have, start identifying patterns or what I call "buckets." For example, if I had written the following as my interests:

- I like to share my experiences with other people
- Interacting with people energizes me
- I would love to help people by sharing my success and failures
- I like giving presentations in meetings and engage the audience
- I would like to help people overcome their stage fright
- I like traveling and meeting new people
- I like to make new friends and grow my network

Then, public speaking is something I would like to do, as it fits all the points. So my first bucket is *public speaking*.

Similarly, identify different buckets that you want to focus your effort and career growth on.

This is called the *Bucket Classification System*. I use this system for all my clients who are stuck in their careers and do not know what their next career path should be.

Stage 2: P—PLAN

A goal without a plan is just a wish. —Antoine de Saint-Exupéry

Now that we have identified different buckets that we want to focus on, the next thing to do is to come up with a plan to achieve your goals under each bucket. There are three key factors to identify and accomplish your goals:

Step 1: *Identify your vision*
Before setting goals, we need to think about our vision. This is the ultimate goal you want to accomplish. It could be becoming a manager, director, senior-level technician, technical lead to anything that you want to aim toward.

To help identify the vision, ask yourselves the following questions:

- What would make you happy in your career?
- Would achieving that goal be meaningful to you?
- Will it make an impact on your life and others around you?
- How do you see yourself several years down the line?
- Does it relate to any buckets you have identified?

For example, at the end of 2016, I identified that *public speaking* was one of my buckets. My vision was *to speak in front of hundreds of people*.

Step 2: *Identify your goals*
Once the vision is identified, the next thing to do is to identify the goals to make that vision come true. These goals could be something you want to accomplish in the next month, quarter, or year. My personal preference is to have yearly goals and then divide that into smaller time frames like months, to make it more manageable.

For example, to make my *speak in front of hundreds of people* vision come true, there were many goals I identified. One of them was to identify a job that would give me more opportunities to speak at conferences and would give me a chance to network with the software testing community.

Step 3: *Identify the tasks to reach your goals*
Once the goal is identified, you need to figure out the different tasks needed to accomplish the goal (which adds up to making your vision become a reality). For example, for my goal of *speaking in front of hundreds of people*, the different tasks I had identified were the following:

- Read books related to giving great presentations
- Record myself speaking to identify areas of strength and improvement
- Research conferences that have large audiences
- Develop session or keynote topics that I can use to apply to those conferences
- Hone my speaking skills by continuing to speak at meetups and smaller conferences

Stage 3: A—ACTION
Now, it is action time. You have identified your vision and goals. It is time to get your butt off the couch and get to work.

For example, following the DPA approach, I was able to identify my ideal job in 2018. I became a Developer Evangelist, doing precisely the work I had wanted to do.

Of course, this was before I figured out that instead of representing one company when I gave talks, I could represent myself and impact more people (which is why I have my own public speaking business now).

Once I identified one of my buckets was *public speaking* way back in 2016, all my work has been focused on this bucket. This helps to give focused attention to the things that are important to you.

My other buckets are *writing* and *coaching*. Yes, you can have multiple buckets because you are a human with multiple interests.

Nine Strategies to Find Your Dream Job

Insanity is doing the same thing over and over again and expecting different results. —Albert Einstein

I speak at various conferences throughout the year and have the chance to meet and network with many different people. One of the most common conversations I have with people is about them trying to find their next job, one that will make them happy and fulfilled. Attendees regularly tell me that they keep applying for jobs, but no one responds to them, and they usually never even receive a call from the company to have a conversation. I ask them whether they tried something different in their job application process since their original strategy is not working. They often respond with a "No" and that they have continued to do the same thing over and over for several months, expecting different results. Let me ask you this: if you want to lose weight, will you continue to eat the same way you have always eaten, which led you to be overweight in the first place or will you do something different to gain control over your health? If you chose the latter option, then you have chosen the right path to make a positive change. So, if you apply this thought process in other areas of your life, why the hell would you not apply it in your career search? Again, remember you spend more than one-third of your life at work, and this is a HUGE deal. Say it with me three times—HUGE, HUGE, HUGE!!! Did that register in your head? If not, repeat it three more times. You may even spend more time at work than with most of your family members.

There are millions of people applying for jobs, thousands applying for similar kinds of positions or roles, and hundreds applying for the same one in the same company. So, if you were one of these folks looking for a job, how would you make your resume stand out from the crowd? How do you make yours unique and set yourself a level higher? This is where the nine strategies I am going to share will help you become an outlier and make companies want you, rather than you wanting them.

Strategy 1: Mind Dump Exercise

Without knowing your destination, it is hard to start. Say you are using Google Maps; if you put in the wrong destination address or in the worst case, no address at all, you are probably not going to get to your destination. Later, there is no point complaining about Google Maps when you created the problem.

Our minds already have all the information about our goals, interests, passion, and motivations. We need to tap into this rich database by strategically writing this information down and making it visible. This is exactly what the mind dump will do. It is an approach to identify the things that you like and hate; then, of course, you can focus on the things you want to do in life.

It works like this:

- Set 30 minutes to an hour of uninterrupted time.
- Download the mind dump template from www.skyrocketyour careerbook.com/resources or simply take a paper and pen.
- Make two columns on the page. In the first column, write down all the things you like to do. When I say all, I really mean *all*. There are no restrictions here; you can write programming, singing, dancing, mentoring, gardening, etc. all in this column—it's not limited to just your profession. In the second column, list things that you dislike doing, following the same process. The point is to write down all the thoughts that are locked in your mind and bring them to the surface.
- From the first column, identify patterns or categories from the things you like to do.
- From those patterns, you can figure out what your ideal job could be and start focusing on that.

DISCOVER YOUR IDEAL CAREER

Things I Love To Do	Things I Hate To Do
_____	_____
_____	_____
_____	_____
_____	_____
_____	_____
_____	_____
_____	_____
_____	_____

For example, if you say:

- *Likes:*

    ☐ *Technical stuff*
    ☐ *To be challenged*
    ☐ *To have authority and freedom over what you do*

- *Dislikes:*

    ☐ *Processes*
    ☐ *Managing teams*
    ☐ *Being micromanaged*

Then maybe your ideal job is to be a software developer at a startup.

Another example could be:
- *Likes:*

- [ ] *Detail oriented*
- [ ] *Seeing the big picture of things*
- [ ] *Communicating with people*
- [ ] *Collaboratively figuring out solutions with different teams*

- *Dislikes:*

  - [ ] *Working in Silos*
  - [ ] *Programming*

Then maybe a scrum master, a business analyst, or a requirement analyst may be the right fit for you.

Whenever I feel lost, overwhelmed with ideas or thoughts, or that I am not accomplishing my goals, I do this exercise and document all of them.

Here is a sample Mind Dump from me

DISCOVER YOUR IDEAL CAREER

Things I Love To Do	Things I Hate To Do
Writing Content	Admin tasks for work
Speaking	Website Maintenance
Mentoring	Customer Support
Programming	Marketing

Download this template and get guidance on how to do this exercise at www.skyrocketyourcareerbook.com/resources.

Strategy 2: Unleash the Power of LinkedIn

LinkedIn is often the most underrated and highly productive social network for professionals. It is really easy to build a network here, and your ideal job may be waiting for you right on the platform. I have completed courses from the top LinkedIn professionals and implemented numerous strategies that have worked with my own LinkedIn profile as well. So, trust me, I know my shit when it comes to LinkedIn.

Update Your Profile

The first step in finding your ideal job is having an updated LinkedIn profile. Every keyword gets indexed by Google and is part of SEO (Search Engine Optimization). All job application websites like Career-Builder, Indeed, Glassdoor, and many others use these keywords to search for candidates like you. So, it is crucial to keep your profile updated. Every position I've landed in the last five years was from my LinkedIn network. It has been nine years since I submitted a resume to find a job. So, everything starts with your LinkedIn profile.

Your Profile Photo

Make sure you have a photo that looks professional and shows you happy and smiling. As humans, we visualize things to build a picture of the other person. It starts with your profile photo. Do not use images with your puppy, significant other, drinking, playing, or anything that you would not submit as a photo to put on a legal document. A simple rule of thumb is to not use any photo which you may likely use on Facebook or Instagram. LinkedIn is a place where professionals hang out, so respect the environment you are in.

Tagline

You need to have a tagline that immediately describes who you are and what you do. For example, my current tagline is "International Keynote Speaker, Writer & Tech Career Coach | Coaching tech people to become successful leaders." From my tagline, people have already started building a picture of me in terms of what I do and what are my areas of expertise and interest. So, make sure to update your tagline, and change it when your interests and career paths change. Keep it short, succinct, and catchy all at the same time. You could say you are a "Technology Advocate | Breaking down barriers between technology through content" or an "Entrepreneur | Helping small businesses make million dollar profits". You get the point.

About

The "About" section is one of the most important parts of your profile. All the information you put in here gets searched on Google and plays into SEO. So, this is where you can shine and exactly convey what you bring to the table. The "About" section should have three kinds of information: (1) what you do, (2) how you make an impact, and (3) what are your skills and strengths. For example, say you are a senior software engineer, your "About" section may look like this:

I am passionate about working for companies that offer fantastic products, services, culture and have a strong mission. I am a full stack developer using my expertise in UX design, customer service, and marketing to build applications that customers want to use. A combination of left-brained and right-brained, I love the challenge of problem solving while discovering creative solutions in visual form. I welcome new experiences, pride myself on being adventurous, and endeavor to always be creative.

Technical Skills:
HTML5, CSS3, Java, JavaScript, React.js, Ember.js, Vue.js, Node.js, SQL, Git, Jasmine, Mocha, Chai, Bootstrap, Python, Swift

Methodologies:
Object-Oriented Programming (OOP), Agile Software Development, Pair-Programming, Test-Driven Development (TDD), Extreme Programming (XP)

Tools:
Adobe Photoshop, Adobe Illustrator, Adobe InDesign, Adobe XD, VS Code, Salesforce, Trello, Asana, JIRA, TestRail

Featured

LinkedIn came up with the featured section to showcase any work you are proud of and want people to know about. This could include articles, videos, publications, or LinkedIn posts that had a lot of comments and views.

Experience

In this section, mention the different job positions you have held throughout your career, along with a description of your responsibilities. When writing the description, ensure you use keywords such as automation, testing, development, trainer, mentoring, leading teams, manager, and programming languages/frameworks you may have used during your tenure at the company. All these keywords get searched by Google and are also rich SEO information, so it's crucial to highlight them. It could help you appear in the top ten results of Google just because you used specific keywords that recruiters, companies, or tools look at to screen candidates. If your industry uses specific language or tools, use those words.

Education

Add all your education-related information in this section. Give a short description of the program and what you accomplished during the time you spent at the university. You can mention your GPA and also any activities, clubs, and organizations you were part of that you think people should know. If you were part of a sorority or fraternity or any other societies, you may include that information in this section as well.

Licenses & Certifications
In this section, showcase all the licenses and certifications you have earned and completed. This section shows that you have decided to invest in your field and taken extra courses to get better at your job. It signifies that you are taking the initiative to learn the skills that companies are looking for in their potential employees. Even if your license has expired, you should include it to indicate that you have learned that information before; the employer may like to know that you once had that certification, whether it is still valid or not.

Volunteer Experience
Companies like people who are involved in extracurricular activities, and many times they specifically like to see people who are volunteering their time to make an impact on the community. Of course, it is generally good to volunteer and serve the community, not just to help you get a job, so start figuring out how you can give back now.

Skills & Endorsements
LinkedIn allows you to add up to 50 skills that are relevant to your field, after that you can mark three of them your top skills by clicking in the pin icon next to the desired skill. Once this is done, you could start asking people to endorse your skills, especially the top three skills that highlight your strengths. A great way to get more endorsements is to endorse other people in your network in exchange for yours. This strategy works like a charm.

Recommendations
This is one of the most crucial sections of your profile. Companies like to know who you are and what they can expect from you if you join their company. One great way to understand what you bring to

the table is to look at your recommendations. This is similar to reading reviews for a movie or book. If you have more positive reviews, it generates more interest. The same strategy you use for getting endorsements applies to recommendations as well.

Accomplishments

If you've got it, flaunt it! In this section, you are going to showcase all your accomplishments in one place, like your articles, blogs, publications, courses, and much more. Also, add the organizations you are affiliated to, which are relevant to the outside world.

EXERCISE

1. Create your LinkedIn profile (if you do not already have one).
2. Ask your friend to take a good picture of you or go to a nearby pharmacy or photo center and get a headshot.
3. Choose a great tagline that reflects who you are and what you do.
4. Update all the sections of your LinkedIn profile based on the instructions in the previous pages.

Tap into Your OWN Network

We spend so much time looking for opportunities and networking with other people in various channels and ignore the obvious and most powerful way of connecting with people—tapping into our own LinkedIn network. You already have connections and people working at various companies, why not just ask them if they know of any jobs that would fit your profile? One of the best parts of doing this is that you get the inside scoop about jobs which haven't gone public yet, so you already are at an advantage compared to other people looking for the same position. For example, if your field of interest is sales, then research who in your network is already working in the company you want to apply for and may have information about sales jobs that interests you. This is one of the most powerful ways to stand out from the crowd and apply for a job before someone else who is better qualified than you does. Also, your contact may receive a referral bonus or be willing to write a recommendation for you to their leadership. This could help bring your resume to the top of the pile for the recruiters.

Cold Messaging

Once you have tapped into your network, the next thing you can do is send messages to people who work in the dream company you want to get a job at. This is where having a LinkedIn Premium subscription helps as you can message people who are not in your network. Of course, there is a strategy for cold messaging as well. Here is a five-step process to do just that:

1. Search for the company you want to work for.
2. Click on the "See all" option of people who work in that company.
3. Start scanning for people who you could cold message. This could be a recruiter, a manager, a mid-level employee, or anyone who you think has the potential to help you get your foot in the door. For example, if I am a senior software engineer, I may try to check out profiles of other senior software engineers, team leads, development managers, or recruiters who work in the same company.
4. Select ONE person from the company who you think is the most likely to respond to a message from you. Be careful not to send messages to multiple people in the company as they do talk to each other, and you don't want them to develop the impression that you are spamming employees.
5. Send a personalized message. Look at their profile and find out what their interests are, where they graduated from, and who are their mutual connections. This will help you to gather some

talking points when you message the person. For example, if you are a data scientist and are looking for a similar opportunity at another company, you may send a message like this: *"Hi, I noticed that you are working on this AI product. I believe my expertise in data science could help make your product better. Could we hop on a quick 15-minute call and discuss some of my ideas?"*

Interview People

Once you find people who have a similar kind of job that you want and are in the company you want to work for, message them and ask whether you could talk to them about the job. For example, say you are looking for a software developer role in a company you like. Search for a person doing software development in that particular company via LinkedIn, or even do a Google search. Then, message the person and request a call with them to talk about their specific job role in the company. More often than not, people are willing to speak to you about their job and help you out. This helps to give you an idea about whether the job is the right fit for you before you waste your or someone else's time.

Strategy 3: Subscribe to Job Alerts

Numerous job websites give information on the latest openings in different companies. The five most popular job websites in the United States are the following:

- Zip Recruiter
- Indeed
- Simply Hired
- Glassdoor
- CareerBuilder
- LinkedIn Jobs

There are many other job websites, but if you have your resume in at least three of the above sites, it would be sufficient to know almost all the jobs. These companies access a shared pool of information, and the majority of the time have the same set of job listings.

To get notified on jobs posted, subscribe to job alerts in each of the above websites. You have settings where you can get daily/weekly emails about jobs that interest you based on the keywords you use. For example, Quality Engineer, QA Manager, UX Designer, Sales Manager are examples of some keywords that you could use to get the specific job you want. Job alerts help to follow a *push approach* where emails automatically get sent to you instead of a *pull approach* where you manually have to search for jobs daily.

You can even generate resumes from LinkedIn itself. This is another reason why you want to update your LinkedIn profile. Most of the job websites give options to upload/make resumes from LinkedIn instead of having to upload a Word or PDF version of your resume. The other advantage of this is not needing to worry about the format or "resume real estate;" your LinkedIn profile can display more detail than you could possibly put on paper, which may be advantageous to employers.

EXERCISE

1. Choose at least three job sites.
2. Create job alerts in each one of them to get daily or weekly emails about job postings.

Strategy 4: Strategize Your Job Application Process

When I applied for 1,293 jobs, I did not know what the hell I was doing. When recruiters called me out of the blue, I did not understand which job they wanted to discuss with me, since I had already applied for about 500 jobs by then. It was hard for me to keep track of what role I had applied for, which company it was with, and when I had submitted the application. I had many situations where I was talking about the wrong job to a recruiter, which, it goes without saying, did not take me further through the interview process.

So, don't be like the 2010 version of me—work smarter not harder. Start strategizing your job application process by following this tracking sheet I specifically created for this purpose. This sheet has different information about the company name, position name, date applied, job link, whether you followed up on the job, any comments you have added, and room to add additional columns. If you have multiple resumes for different kinds of jobs, specify which resume you sent out. One thing to highlight here is that it is essential to follow up on all jobs you apply for. This is what separates you from the other applicants. Usually, you should do the follow-ups about five days after you submitted the application. It will help to show the recruiter that you are interested in the job, and you are putting in the extra effort into getting to know more about it.

Download the job tracking sheet here: www.skyrocketyourcareerbook.com/resources

Strategy 5: Attend Meetups and Networking Events

Meetups and other networking events are a great way to develop new connections and find your dream job. These events attract many different kinds of people, and the opportunities are endless. Below are some strategies that I have followed to get the best out of these events:

- Search for events that are relevant to your field.
- After you register for the event, research the attendees. Usually, these events will show a list of people attending the event. Go through every name from the event website, and search it on LinkedIn. You will often get a complete profile of where they work and what they do. Make a note of people who are working in a job which you are interested in.

- During the event, make sure to meet these people in person, and ask them about the company and their job.

If you have the right attitude and cordially approach them, they are generally willing to help you out and even serve as a referral in the company that has your ideal job. Not many people do this, but it is a gold mine to get new contacts and opportunities.

Strategy 6: Invest in Yourself

If I did not spend $3,000 of my own money to attend a conference in 2011, I would never have become an international keynote speaker, nor would I be writing this book. If I did not decide to move from Cleveland, Ohio, to Chicago, Illinois, I would have never discovered new opportunities, friends, and interests. My wife's Grandma Ruth used to call this "divine discontent." When the universe is giving us signs to make a change, it is up to us to welcome and embrace it with open arms.

If you are not mentally and physically happy, it is exceptionally difficult to make others around you happy. When you do not focus on yourself, instead of spreading positive energy, you will be giving out negative energy to other people. The only way to grow and nurture your body, mind, and spirit is to invest in yourself. We are all works in progress, but what makes you and me different from other people is that we put in the effort to improve and strive for greatness continually.

Start listening to podcasts, reading books, taking online courses, and seeking out mentors/coaches. One of the biggest changes to my mental health was when I began meditating and practicing mindfulness—you may also find that they can help you take control of your mind. Exercise regularly, and treat your body with respect. All these things add up to make you more productive, more receptive to new ideas, and find opportunities for growth.

It ain't where you start in life, it's what you do in life, that determines where you end up in life. —Colin Powell

Strategy 7: Start Your Side Hustle

If you are like me, you have either thought about starting something on your own but just don't know what it is yet, or you have started your side hustle and are looking to make it into your primary job. In early 2016, I decided I wanted to do something on my own, but I was scared of change, nervous about the amount of work I would have to take on. Also, I had a cushy 9–5 job, so I was even less motivated. So, I put it in the parking lot, thinking I will get to it later. But what happened was that the thought of starting something new was running through my head almost daily, even if I did not want to think about it. The entrepreneurial itch, spirit, virus, or whatever you want to call it is real. Once you catch it, it is hard to let go. So, don't think that putting away the thought of starting something will help you to continue your usual way of life. It will start eating you up daily when you do not act on your instincts.

In mid-2017, I finally registered my company and started my side hustle. My initial goal was to do training and workshops on the side, while I still had my high-paying, full-time job. But in early 2019, I realized that I was more passionate about speaking, writing, and coaching people to help them lead better lives by getting them their dream job. So, I pivoted and rebranded my company and business model. What I am saying here is that even if you start a side hustle, it does not mean you will be doing that particular job permanently. You can always pivot and try other things as you learn and grow through your entrepreneurial journey. This is the beauty of entrepreneurship.

There are seven steps to start your side hustle:

1. Figure out your strengths though the Mind Dump exercise. (Go back to *strategy 1* for more info.)
2. Research how you can use those strengths to help people.
3. Write down all the ideas to impact people, and pick the top three.

4. Identify what problem you can solve.
5. Identify your audience.
6. Create your service.
7. Market and promote your service.

An easy filtering process to figure out your side hustle is to ask yourself these three fundamental questions:

- What makes you excited to wake up in the morning?
- What part of your work do you love? What part makes you happy when you do it?
- What is going to make an impact on your and other people's lives?

Finally, make sure you identify your niche and service offering in such a way that it is clear to you and your audience. For example: I am not a Life Coach, Business Coach, Relaxation Coach, Fitness Coach, or Spiritual Coach. I am a Tech Career Coach. I help tech folks land their dream job and become successful leaders. This is what I do. This may change in the future, but for now, I am clear on whom I am serving. So make sure you clearly identify your niche.

Strategy 8: Keep Yourself Motivated

We are constantly surrounded by negativity. You may have family and friends who are jealous of your growth and try to pull you down. Don't focus on these people; try to surround yourself with positive energy and thoughts.

Some strategies to keep yourself motivated are as follows:
- *Read inspirational quotes*: I am a sucker for inspirational quotes. I surround my home and office with printouts and pictures of quotes that keep me motivated at all times. We are human, and we are going to feel shitty at some point or the other. During those times, you can use these inspirational quotes to motivate you and get you back on track to achieve your goals. Check out

my list of inspirational quotes here: www.skyrocketyourcareer-book.com/resources

- *Keep your goals visible*: The reason why most people fail to reach their goals is that they do not keep them visible. There's a reason why most New Year resolutions are thrown out by February. We are visual people and need to see things to remind ourselves of our purpose and mission on a daily basis. I print my goals and put them in various locations in my home, including my office and bedroom. This forces me to see these goals daily and reminds me to keep progressing.

- *Read motivational books*: Just like how exercise is the fuel for the body, books are the fuel for the mind. As you read motivational books, your mind will be trained to think positively. Dr. Seuss, the famous children book author, said, *The more that you read, the more things you will know. The more that you learn, the more places you'll go.*

- *Listen to podcasts*: When you are on a walk, working out, or even doing house chores, listen to an inspiring podcast to set the tone for the day.

- *Watch TED talks*: There are so many inspirational talks on TED that have millions of views for a reason. Whenever you feel you need a break from work or personal life, check out a TED talk.

- *Seek mentors/coaches*: There are already people who have gone through a similar kind of journey as the one you want to go on. Why not just reach out to them and ask about their failures and successes? You do not have to make mistakes to become experienced; you can learn from other people's mistakes as well. In the past decade, I had exponential growth simply because I had mentors and coaches helping me grow. Instead of me trying to figure everything out, they advised me on what to do and what not to do.

- *Have accountability partners*: Studies have shown that accountability partners increase your chances of success by 95 percent.

It could be your trusted friend, mentor, coach, or anyone who is going or has gone through the same journey as you, who would keep you accountable.

Strategy 9: Mindset Shift

Our minds are crazy and fascinating at the same time. While our body and soul tells us one thing, the mind can do a total 180-degree turn and make you do something against your wishes. So how do we prevent this repetitive cycle from happening? How can we master our minds? I am not going to focus on meditation here, although it has tremendously helped me gain mastery of my mind, but rather I wanted to highlight the power of positive reframing.

All the things that happen to us are temporary. For example, we may be living in a situation that is causing havoc in our lives, but remember that it is going to end, and a new phase or era will begin. Global pandemics, the 9/11 attacks, the Anthrax scare, 2008 Recession—they all seemed like they would go on forever, but of course, another event or phase came along to change our focus. While many were affected by these unfortunate incidents and for some, they were life-altering, most of us survived the situations and continued with our regular life, albeit with adaptation. In the future, we are going to have a lot more shit to deal with, but remember, it is temporary. No matter what happens, life moves on; time does not stop and continues to tick. So, are you going to sit and bitch about the past or take a bold step into the future and pursue your dreams?

Controlling your mind starts with positive reframing. In any stressful situation, think about the positive factors that have come out of it. Even in the global COVID-19 pandemic situation, people started appreciating the little things in life we took for granted, like family, friends, groceries, health, internet, video conferencing, and much more. This is what I am talking about when I say positive reframing.

In my own life, there have been many difficult situations, one of which was losing my grandma to cancer. She was very dear to me, and she suffered through so much pain and agony before her death. She was my confidant, friend, well-wisher, guide, and role model when it comes to positive thinking. I still think of her and am grateful she taught me to be a kind person and to help people, and see the good things in any problematic situation. I carry these values with me since she passed away.

Remember, as Kyle Cease said, *In life, everything happens for you, not to you.*

I would not have accomplished all the things I currently have if I did not shift my mindset from a place of scarcity to a place of abundance. I spent the last 15 years researching, learning, and implementing different strategies that could help me find the best career for me and my true passion. I have dedicated the majority of my life to finding out key factors that could exponentially boost productivity and peak performance. I apply these learnings when coaching my clients on how to find their dream jobs and be successful in the career of their choice.

About 75 percent of my coaching clients come to me when they are earning five-figure salaries. They usually are low on confidence, have low self-esteem, high self-doubt, and do not believe in themselves at first. But after I use my experience and strategies to show them how to shift their mindset, they start earning upper six-figure salaries. This is what I usually tell them: "If you think you are worth $50k, then your actions and work will reflect a person who is worth $50k, but if you think you are worth $100k or $500k, your actions and mindset will reflect a person who is making that much."

It is all about building your brand and showing up every single day, irrespective of the circumstances.

There is never a right time to start anything. The right time is NOW.

Everything will be okay in the end. If it is not okay, it's not the end. — John Lennon

SUMMARY OF CHAPTER 1

Nine strategies to get your dream job:
- Strategy 1: Mind Dump exercise

  - Unlock the thoughts in your mind and identify what you like and dislike doing.

- Strategy 2: Unleash the Power of LinkedIn

  - Update your LinkedIn profile.
  - Tap into your own network.
  - Cold message people with personalized messages.

- Strategy 3: Subscribe to Job Alerts

  - Use keywords related to your job, and subscribe to get daily/weekly notifications right to your inbox.

- Strategy 4: Strategize Your Job Application Process

  - Use the job application tracking sheet, and control your job application from start to finish.

- Strategy 5: Attend Meetups and Networking Events

  - Meetups and other networking events are a great way to develop new connections and find your dream job.

- Strategy 6: Invest in Yourself

  - The biggest gift you can give yourself is to invest in yourself to grow your mind, body, and soul. Be selfish and take care of yourself first and others second.

- Strategy 7: Start Your Side Hustle

- Follow the seven steps to start your side hustle.

- Strategy 8: Keep Yourself Motivated

  - Reduce negativity and have different ways to keep yourself motivated.

- Strategy 9: Mindset Shift

  - Use the power of positive reframing and successfully handle difficult situations.

CHAPTER 2
How to Ace Interviews and Negotiate Salary

*If you were able to believe in Santa Claus for like 8
years, you can believe in yourself for 5 minutes.*
—Unknown

Strategies to Ace Interviews

Back in my undergraduate days, I was a nervous wreck. The thought
of talking to someone who had endless rights to judge me for who I
am and what I bring to the table in a short amount of time made me
want to vomit before an interview. Sometimes, I think that it is not fair
that a group of people get to make judgments on me based on one to
two hours of discussion, but in their defense, they have shit to do in
life, and interviewing me is not high up on their priority list. So, they
do it as part of their job—sometimes out of interest, and sometimes
out of compulsion. Whatever be the case, this is the reality, and we
just have to go with it.

After attending hundreds of interviews as a candidate and conduct-
ing many more, I started observing common patterns in candidates.
I analyzed all these interviews and noted down what makes people
succeed and fail. I also started reading books and listening to podcasts
on interviews. Based on this research, I identified eight strategies that
will help anyone ace any kind of interview.

Eight Strategies to Conquer Interviews

Strategy 1: Research the Company

It is vital to research the company you are interviewing for. The worst thing you could do to jeopardize your interview is to not know anything about the company and stare at the interviewers when they ask a question like "What do you like about our company?" or "What product teams within our company would you be interested in working on?"

Of course, this is an opportunity to show off your curiosity and interest in working for the company. Research the company's products, services, and any recent announcements they made that were publicized by the media or press releases. Make a note of all this information, and use it for small talk during interviews. This also helps to make the interviewers know that you are proactive and interested to work at the company.

Strategy 2: Research the Interviewers

How do you connect with people? How can you quickly start a conversation with someone you haven't met before? My wife can chat up anyone and everyone in less than a minute, and get them talking about their lives in less than five. But, if you're not from the Midwest like her, the answer is to research the fuck out of their social profile to get to know their interests before you meet them. This same technique can be used for first dates, too. Another thing I learned from my wife.

For job interviews, look primarily into the LinkedIn profile of the person who is going to interview you, if you know their names. They would have mentioned their interests, specialty, what they are currently working on, where they graduated from, and other topics. Identify some key points from their profile, and use that as a conversation starter when you meet them. For example, if I found out that my interviewer went to the Ohio State University, I would immediately note this down, and when I meet them, I would start a conversation about football or basketball. Go Buckeyes!!! Another example would be if you noticed your interviewer had done research on AI in her master's program, then you could brush up on some primary AI keywords you could use during your conversation with her. Realize that interviewers are humans like us and would like to get to know you on a personal level, especially if they may be hiring you for their own team.

Strategy 3: The 90-day Plan

This is a framework used to onboard new employees, but it can be helpful during job interviews as well. You research the company and figure out what are the different things you can accomplish in the first 90 days after you join the company. This does not need to be exact; it could be anything you feel you could contribute to the team in the first 90 days.

Now, why is this important? Let me start with this: how many of you have ever done a 90-day plan for a job interview? For most of the people reading this book, the answer would be NEVER. So, there you go, not many people use this for interviews. If you do a 90-day plan, you already have the edge over other candidates as you are showing curiosity, interest, and ability to go "above and beyond" for the job. Interviewers recognize this and remember it. The key is to differentiate yourself from hundreds of other candidates, and this approach is pure gold as its value is exponential in getting you the job.

There are various ways you can make a 90-day plan: Word, Excel, PowerPoint. But, my favorite is to use mind maps as it can show everything in one single page in a visually pleasing and understandable format. Below is a mind map I used for a software testing interview, and I got the job. For the purpose of the book, I have customized the original version to make it more generic for all audiences of this book just so that you can understand how it works. Download my sample 90-day plan here: www.skyrocketyourcareerbook.com/resources

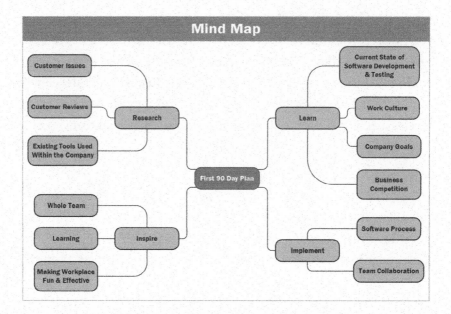

Strategy 4: Make Everything about You (the Hook Technique)

The most significant mistake people make during interviews is that they answer a specific question but fail to use specific keywords in their reply that could steer the conversation toward a topic that they are already familiar with.

For example, say, you are asked, "Tell me about a situation where you had a big problem, and you successfully solved it?" You could answer this question in two ways:

Answer 1: "A couple of years ago, we had a huge customer issue, where our banking application kept crashing when customers tried to upgrade to the newer version of the app. The way I was able to solve this was......(you give the solution you came up with)." Then you stop your reply.

Answer 2: "A couple of years ago, we had a huge customer issue, where our banking application kept crashing when customers tried to upgrade to the newer version of the app. The way I was able to solve this was...(you give the solution you came up with)." Then you continue the conversation, saying something like "This is why they call me the *therapist* in the team. Whenever there are difficult conversations that need to be had, my manager calls me to fix the issue as I am a *good listener* and let people vent, then try to solve the problem with empathy."

What is the difference between answers 1 and 2? In the former, I reply to the answer. In the latter, I respond and add extra information about how I am a good listener, have empathy, and a problem-solving attitude. I wanted to add something interesting that the interviewer would notice.

This is called the *hook*. You need to cast hooks whenever you reply to questions. Once they bite, you steer the conversation toward something you already know and talk about it for a while. Make the interview all about you, and try to massage the questions asked to match things you already know.

If you used the hook technique, the follow-up question to answer 2 may go like this:

The interviewer notices the hook and asks, "Wow, they gave you the nickname "therapist?" That is interesting." Then I reply by saying, "Yeah, it took me a lot of time to get better at difficult conversations, but once I started practicing being a good listener and leading with empathy, it dramatically changed my life. This is why I was voted the *star performer* last year as I was able to resolve a lot of issues before they blew up into bigger ones."

Did you notice what I did now? I added another hook: "star performer." Now, the conversation can steer toward you being a star performer, or at least, the interviewer makes a note of this.

Just in two replies, I let the interviewer know multiple data points about my personality and work. This is the hook technique.

It took me several years to master this technique, but the more you prepare, attend, and conduct interviews, the more experience you will get in using and casting hooks. You can apply the hook strategy not only in interviews but in any conversations you have, especially in new environments, to make you the focal point of everything.

As I said before, if you've got it, flaunt it.

Strategy 5: Ask Clarifying Questions

Interview questions can get really weird, like "How many stoplights are there in the United States?" or "How many gas stations are needed in the United States?" or abstract questions like "What is the ultimate answer to life, the universe, and everything?" (In case you were wondering, the answer is 42. It is from the book *The Hitchhiker's Guide to the Galaxy*; yes, I am a nerd, and I am fucking proud of it.) You may not get this question in the interview, but the point is that interview questions can get weird.

When in doubt, ask clarifying questions before you give your answer. You could say things like the following:

- "Could you repeat the question, please?"
- "When you say X, do you mean Y?"
- "Am I allowed to make some assumptions about your question like…?"
- "Do you want an exact number, or could I tell you the approximate value?"

Interviewers appreciate the fact that you are trying to get clarity before you answer. This shows that you are an effective thinker and communicator.

Strategy 6: Prepare Elevator Pitch for Common Questions

An elevator pitch is a short description of anything that can quickly explain something in an understandable format. This is usually used to pitch an idea for a company or product, or explaining your job description to others.

When it comes to interviews, you need to have an elevator pitch for the most commonly asked questions. Some examples could be the following:

- What are your strengths?
- What are your weaknesses?
- Why do you want to work for our company?
- What made you apply for this job?
- Tell me about a time where you solved a complex issue, and how you handled it.
- Tell me about a time where you tried something, and it failed. How did you handle the situation?
- Give me an example of a difficult conversation you had to have with a coworker. How did you resolve it?
- When you work, do you like structure or are you fine with handling things as they come to you?
- What is the reason you are leaving your current/previous company?
- Why is there a gap between your previous job and now? (Or any other large gaps in your work history.)

Of course, these are just the heavy-hitters—there are a ton of commonly asked questions in an interview, so make sure you prepare. Once you can answer these questions efficiently in your sleep, then you are ready; of course, you can use the same answer and tweak it for other questions you did not prepare for.

Check out more commonly asked questions during interviews here: www.skyrocketyourcareerbook/resources

Strategy 7: Check the Tone of Your Voice and Your Body Language

I admit that I fidget. I am the type of person who cannot sit in one place for more than 45 minutes to an hour. Daily, I practice deep work, i.e., focused work on one particular task. Each session is for an hour, and after that, I take a break to drink water, do ten pushups, then start my next deep work session. (For more information about deep work, check out Cal Newport's book of the same name.) The point here is, I need movement. Strike that out. I actually crave movement and physical activity.

Until about five years ago, I used to keep shaking my leg and rocking my body back and forth in meetings, interviews, and video calls. In one of the interviews, the interviewer could not handle my restlessness and called me out on it. Since that embarrassing incident, I have always been conscious of my body movements in public. (My wife also made me very aware of it and brings it to my attention if I slip. I've been known to shake cars with my leg bouncing at stoplights.) Also, I used to frown a lot when I was listening intently. This was perceived negatively in meetings. Because while I grew up in India, I didn't realize this was something specific to Indians. I also used to do the infamous "head bobble." Instead of shaking the head left and right, or nodding it up and down to signify yes or no, we Indians shake our heads side-to-side like we are stretching our neck muscles in either direction. This confuses the heck out of most non-Indians as he/she does not know whether the "bobber" is agreeing or disagreeing with something. Unfortunately, this is a cause of confusion in interviews as well. So, be aware of your body language, including head movements. (Also, for those of you that aren't Indian, my wife had a breakthrough a few years ago when she realized that the head bob usually means a reluctant "yes." There you go, the hidden gem of insight in this book.)

Another aspect to pay attention to is the tone of voice. Remember, you are usually in a small room when you attend interviews, and they are pretty soundproof. This means that the more sound you make, the louder it gets in the room. I am a loud guy. In half of my conferences, I do not even use a mic, and still, the person in the hundredth row can hear me well. But, when I am in a small room, I need to watch my tone of voice to ensure I am not too loud. This also applies to the way you reply to questions. Just be calm, composed, and not too loud, but if your interviewer looks like they're straining to hear you, then make sure to speak loud enough so they can hear you and all the reasons they should hire you.

Strategy 8: Ask Great Questions

You always need to prepare smart, useful, and thought-provoking questions before an interview. After every interview, the interviewers are going to ask you this: "Do you have any questions for us?" And the answer should always be YES.

Asking great questions shows people your eagerness about the job and enthusiasm to work at the company. Follow this process to ask outstanding questions:

Figure out how many interviews you are attending that day. On average, you need about three questions for every interview. So, if you have four interviews, the number of questions would be? 4x3 = 12 questions. Sorry, I did not want to bother you with math, but I was just giving you an idea. So, prepare a set of questions that you want to ask at the end of each interview, using the information you may have gotten from strategies 1 and 2. Sometimes, you may have time to get through all of your prepared questions, but sometimes you won't. Gauge how much time is left at the end of the interview, and ask questions accordingly.

Also, make sure you do not ask the same set of questions to each interviewer if you are having a series of interviews for a particular job on a given day. The interviewers regroup and talk about you at the end of the day, so you don't want to come off as the person who had the exact same set of questions for each interviewer. It feels weird.

● ● ● ●

Salary Negotiation

Oh, the dreaded salary negotiation process! You follow the strategies outlined in this book and nail the interview. You get the job offer, and you are jumping up and down in joy. Then you open the job offer and realize you need to address the elephant in the room, i.e., how much are you going to get paid for the shit you are going to do for the company?

Research suggests that less than half of the population negotiates their salaries.[2] This is fucking crazy! I am going to break this to you: companies do not give a shit about the amount they are going to pay you. The reality is, they have enough money to pay you for that position, and that is the reason they are interviewing you in the first place. They have already done their research from PayScale, Glassdoor, and other websites about the minimum, median, and maximum salaries companies pay for the open position. So, it is only fair that you do an equal amount of research and show you cannot be taken advantage of.

I started in the minimum salary range when I joined the workforce. After a while, I increased my salary by over 150 percent. Yes, that is right, freaking 150 percent. Some people I've worked with have increased their salaries 400 percent since I started coaching and guiding them! This is because I not only put in the effort to be a rockstar but also negotiated my salary and benefits since I knew what I was worth. I had confidence in myself, and I was not going to let others dictate my monetary value. So the first step to being successful is to believe that you are worth a certain amount of money based on your skill sets, market value, and the company you are applying to.

The Art of Salary Negotiation

Salary negotiation is a conversation based on facts rather than emotional and irrational assumptions about what you or the company thinks is going to work out. It is a process where you try to understand

---

[2]   "Starting Salary: Negotiable or Not?—Feb 5, 2018—Robert Half." 5 Feb. 2018, http://rh-us.mediaroom.com/2018-02-05-Starting-Salary-Negotiable-or-Not.

what the company can offer you, match it with your expectations, and figure out a common ground where both you and the company could be happy. This is why it is called a "negotiation," and not a "confrontation," "fight," "battle," or any other word that could signify conflict.

Here are the most common mistakes job seekers make when it comes to getting the salary they want versus what they are offered:

Reveal Their Current Salary

Never ever reveal your current salary. The reason is, you may be getting a lower wage at your current job compared to the market value for the amount of effort you are putting in for the work. So, if you mention your current salary to your new employer, you have already set expectations on what your base salary should be, and it is difficult to get a substantial increase during negotiation. Also, in some states, it is illegal to ask you how much you make. So, what if the company still asks you the dreaded question: *How much do you make currently?*

First of all, they want to be able to low-ball you, and it is a dick move. But, if you feel the company is still an excellent fit for you, let go of your ego, and say you are making at least 15–20 percent more than your current salary. Secondly, remember you're trying to get more, and you want to make sure you weren't being underpaid in your current position.

Give a Specific Number for Expected Salary

A common question a recruiter is going to ask you is "What are your salary expectations for the job?" More often than not, people give a specific number. This is a big mistake. What if the company was willing to pay you a lot higher in the first place? You just shot yourself in the foot by giving them a number lower than what they would pay, which is way more affordable and cheap for them. Whenever you get these questions, answer in ranges.

How to arrive at ranges?

Step 1: *Look at a cost of living calculator*
A cost of living calculator helps to give you an idea of how much money you would have to make to live a decent life. You can also compare between cities so that if you are planning on moving somewhere, you can see how much you should make to lead a comparable life to what you are now. Some websites that provide this information are the following:

- NerdWallet
- Bankrate
- CNN money
- PayScale

Step 2: *Find out salary ranges for your job*
Websites like Glassdoor and PayScale give you information on the minimum, median, and maximum salary you can get for a given job in a given location. This helps to know how much you are worth and what you need to be earning at your next job.

Once you have sufficient information by following step 1 and 2, you know the range of salary that you will be comfortable with.

So, when asked the question about salary expectations, first say that you expect something that you are comfortable with, taking into consideration your experience, skill set, and cost of living. If they further push you to give them a number, just say, "Based on my research, I expect a salary between $x and $y." Remember, your $x amount should be 15–20 percent more than what you are already getting. Your $y amount should be more than the maximum value your job should pay.

Follow the "Multiple Offer" Rule

Have you ever bought a car? If so, have you had this situation before: You go to multiple car dealers and get a quote for the car you want. Once you pick a dealership you want to buy the car from, you go there and ask them *what they can do to match the offer of another dealer?* Sometimes, this may be true, where another dealership is offering you a better price but a shittier customer experience. Still, many times you just give the impression that you have multiple offers and make the dealerships fight with each other to get your business. First of all, if you haven't haggled over car pricing, shame on you because you can save a lot of money. Secondly, I am Asian, so keeping up with the stereotypes, I am going to try to get the best pricing possible.

Well, the same situation applies to salary negotiation as well. This is called the *Multiple Offer Rule*. When a company decides to give you a job offer because you are awesome, you may have also interviewed with multiple other companies and gotten other job offers too. This is a golden situation to be in as you can make the companies fight for you.

You can tell one company that you are getting a better offer and perks and ask them to match that offer. Sometimes this may be true, but other times, even if you do not have other job offers, you tell them that you have another job offer and use that in your salary negotiation process. They cannot legally ask you which company you got a job offer from, and you are under no obligation to reveal it. Despite that, if they ask you, just say another tech company and stop. You don't have to explain yourself.

I know what you are thinking now: *Oh no! What if they decide to rescind my job offer because of asking this question?* First of all, understand this, the company has already invested time, effort, and money on you. They go through the process of coming up with a job description, then letting the public know about it, hiring a recruiting agency to help them out, then interviewing many candidates, which means the employees have to spend time on interviews, which means they are not spending time on actual work, which means they are getting paid for not doing the original job they were hired to do. This means the company is paying a steep price for finding the right candidate. Do you see where I am going with this? Giving you the job offer is the final stage of a cumbersome and painstaking process. So, they are not going to take back your job offer. This has never happened in my life or anyone I have ever known in the IT industry for the past 15 years. Of course, if this situation ever happens, then the company is not the right fit for you. You do not want to work in a company where the culture is bad, and they are probably going to treat you like shit. This is what in my dictionary I call a dick move: a company deciding to take back your offer for asking for money you deserve.

Many people I have coached and helped are afraid to ask for more money, thinking it is something terrible. Remember, this is your fucking life; if you are not going to fight for more money to help provide more income for your family, then who will? Let that sink in a little bit before you move on.

That said, the way you approach this situation matters. You don't have to raise your voice, be fearful, or be nervous when you ask them to match the offer of another company. They understand that this is a normal situation and more often than not, try to see what they can do about it. Remember, they want you, and that is why they gave you the job offer in the first place.

So, be bold, be brave, and follow the *Multiple Offer Rule*. I have exponentially increased my salary by following this approach.

Money Is Not Everything

Do you know you can negotiate for more things other than just money? Yes, I did not think we could do that until I tried it in my last few jobs. When it comes to salary, we immediately think it has to be a base salary and the bonus package. But, other perks are sometimes more valuable than money.

Vacation Days

While many companies are offering "unlimited" vacation packages, some of them still have predefined amounts of vacation and sick days employees can take, just like old times. I personally prefer a set number of vacation days instead of unlimited vacation, as I have control over how I use my vacation days. For companies having an unlimited vacation policy, there is usually a catch: you can take those days off only if the manager approves it or if the project is not busy, or else you may need to find someone to cover your work during those days. Also, the companies that have this policy do not have to pay the employees for unused PTO (paid time off) if they leave the company. Nowadays, it is more of a marketing gimmick to attract talent.

Research has shown[3] that employees take a fewer or equal number of vacation days when there is an unlimited vacation policy compared to having a set amount of days to use. As they feel guilty that they are taking advantage of the perk, they are nervous about getting approval or find it hard to track how many days they are taking off in a year. So, do not fall into the trap of the "unlimited" vacation policy, as it is not necessarily a perk.

That being said, if a company does offer predefined PTO and sick leave, you ask them to increase the number by a week or two as part of the negotiation purpose. This is worth more than money as you get to spend time with your family and also get 100 percent paid during that time. Let me paint the picture for you: Say your desired salary range is between $100k–$115k. After a couple of rounds of salary negotiation, you find out the maximum the company can offer you is a salary of $105k and two weeks of PTO. You can then request them to increase your vacation days by a week to three weeks.

Best of all, you do not need to work during these paid vacation days. So, an increase in vacation days is a better deal than an increase in base salary.

---

[3]   "For millennials, unlimited vacation isn't always a perk." 10 Sep. 2019, https://www.fastcompany.com/90398810/for-millennials-unlimited-vacation-isnt-always-a-perk.

Companies like Buffer and HubSpot have a minimum vacation day policy. This means you need to take a certain amount of days off every year. How cool is that?

So, choose the offer wisely and negotiate on vacation days.

Perks

Companies have different perks to attract talent. Google, Facebook, and many other companies have free food, fitness centers, and much more. But employees end up working for more than 10 hours/day at least, between their free company bus commute, which is equipped with high-speed Wi-Fi, and the time they spend at the company. This reminds me of how we raise chickens: provide them with vast pasture land, with a lot of nutritious food, just so that the farmer can use its eggs and the chicken itself for food. The chicken does not know this yet. But, we are not fucking chickens, so wake the fuck up and realize what companies are doing to you when they offer perks.

When offered perks as part of the job offer, evaluate them wisely. Do the math to see whether they are really worth it or if there is an ulterior motive behind them. If the perks the company offers are of no value to you, then just say that clearly to the recruiter or hiring manager, and negotiate on salary and vacation days. Be open and frank as this is your fucking money.

In my previous companies, I negotiated work from home days. I considered this as a significant perk as I had a regular 9–5 job where I had to go into the office. But the world changed with the COVID-19 pandemic, and this may not be relevant anymore for employees. I still wanted to mention that if the company allows you to work remotely only once a week, then you can negotiate to make it three times a week and make them add that line to your offer letter. I did this in the past, and it gave me a lot of flexibility.

Finally, you can ask them to cover some of your commuting and personal expenses, like gas, train ticket, cell phone bill, internet bill, and so on.

Job Title

I think in this day and age, job titles do not matter anymore. I have worked with people who have an Arts degree who were great at IT and were my managers, to people who had a Masters in Computer Science who never really got the hang of coding. I think only the experience and ability to learn matter, not the title.

This being said, sometimes it may help to have a better job title, especially if you decide to switch companies after a couple of years. It helps in easier salary negotiation and looks good on your resume. For example, "Director of Engineering" sounds and looks better than "Engineering Manager." "CTO" sounds and looks better than the "VP of Technology."

If the company offers you a job, keep in mind that you can ask them to modify the name of the job title, which you think will look better for your future growth. Many companies would be open to making that change, again since they have already spent enough time and money in interviewing you.

Hopefully, you now realize that there are so many ways and options to negotiate your salary. Your base salary is just one part of the whole equation to get the money you deserve. Just because a company has not offered something to other employees does not mean they cannot make an exception for you. You are different—believe in that—and get the offer you feel reflects your worth.

Finally, make sure every fucking thing gets written in the offer letter before you sign it. I have been burned in the past when companies verbally agreed upon something, but once I joined, the circumstances made them go back on their previous commitments.

SUMMARY OF CHAPTER 2

Eight strategies to ace interviews

- Strategy 1: Research the Company

    - Before the interview, research the company's products, services, and any recent announcements they made.

- Strategy 2: Research the Interviewers

    - Find out who is interviewing, and research their social media profiles, mainly LinkedIn.

- Strategy 3: The 90-day Plan

    - Be proactive and show up prepared to show what you feel you will accomplish in the first 90 days after joining the company. Download my sample 90-day plan here: www.skyrocketyourcareerbook.com/resources.

- Strategy 4: Make Everything about You (the Hook Technique)

    - Use specific keywords in your replies to steer the conversations to things you already know while highlighting your skills.

- Strategy 5: Ask Clarifying Questions

    - If you do not understand the question, ask for clarification. Interviewers appreciate the effort.

- Strategy 6: Prepare Elevator Pitch for Common Questions

    - Research common questions that are asked during job interviews for your position, and prepare to answer them with clarity. A list of commonly asked interview questions can be found here: www.skyrocketyourcareerbook.com/resources.

- Strategy 7: Check the Tone of Your voice and Your Body Language

  - Be mindful of your voice and body language during interviews. It can be distracting to the interviewers.

Strategy 8: Ask Great Questions

  - Prepare at least three questions to ask at the end of each interview.

Salary Negotiation
- Less than half of the people negotiate salaries. You are giving away free money.
- The Art of Salary Negotiation:

  - Salary negotiation is a conversation. The best result is a win-win situation for both the sides.
  - Common mistakes during the negotiation:

    ☐ Revealing your current salary.
    ☐ Giving a specific number for expected salary.

- Money Is Not Everything

  - Negotiate on vacation days, perks, and job title.

CHAPTER 3
Becoming Successful at Your Dream Job

· ·

Whether you think you can or think you can't, you're right.
—Henry Ford

Believe in Yourself

It was the first week of September 2008. I went on a tour of my campus at Rochester Institute of Technology (RIT). It was beautiful. I had never seen such magnificent buildings and huge campuses. Remember, I came from India, and our universities were not that developed yet. I went to my department's building, which was Software Engineering, and made a note of where the labs were, who my professors were going to be, where the classes were held; it was exciting. I could not wait to start. I had come to the United States with a big dream, and this was my time. I could feel it.

Classes started in the second week of September 2008. Back then, RIT was following the quarter system where there were four 10-week sessions, each held in the fall, winter, spring, and summer. (In 2013, they moved to a semester system, where they have two 15-week sessions). It was rare for students to take more than three courses every quarter, as the workload was intense due to cramming 15 weeks' worth of lessons in 10 weeks. This was especially true if you were enrolled in an engineering program. But, like many other immigrants, I ended up taking four courses each quarter due to two reasons: (1) You could finish your Master's program earlier and (2) You get the fourth course free. So you get four courses for the price of three. What a bargain to a thrifty Indian!

My first incident which tested my newly established belief system and self-confidence (after my undergrad experience) happened three weeks into my first quarter. One of my professors called me in his office. He said he noticed in his class that I was not smart enough to complete the program compared to the other students, and that I did not have the right aptitude for learning. He told me it would be good for everyone if I dropped out of the course, as there was no way I was passing it. He said that at the rate I was performing, I was going to fail his course with an F grade. This came as a complete shock to me as I thought I was doing well. I left his office, went to an empty room, and cried. I could not believe what had just happened, and my emotional and mental confidence broke. That entire night, I did not sleep as I was thinking to myself: *I cannot drop out of the course, change my degree, and go back to where I came from. I came to pursue my master's and had a dream. So, was I going to quit the program or figure out some other solution to mitigate this issue?*

I gave it a lot of thought and told myself that I am enough, I matter, and I can do whatever it takes to get to the next level. So, I decided not to drop out of either that course or the program. To cut a long story short, I worked my butt off and not only managed to pass that professor's course with a B grade, but ended up getting all A's in all of my other courses for my entire master's program. This whole experience showed me that the power to make a difference is within me. It taught me that things are temporary, and shit happens, but the way we react to the circumstances is what makes the difference. If you are focused on your goals and want to get to the next level, you need to do whatever it takes to reach it.

Since then, I have had several incidents that shook my belief system, but I kept fighting through every obstacle that came my way, and I remembered that life happens. Life does not care about race, religion, gender, or social, mental, or physical status; it happens whether you like it or not. We control our actions, and our goals and mission guide our actions.

Things are never as bad as they feel or as good as they sound. —Unknown

Six strategies to Be Successful at Your Dream Job

Now you got your dream job. Yaay! It is time for a celebration. My advice is, try to delay the start of your new job for as long as possible. This is the time to go on a vacation, have a staycation, give yourself a break, release some steam, and try to rejuvenate before your next job.

After the vacation is over and it's your first day at your new job, what do you do? How do you ensure that you are going to be successful in your new role in your new company? First of all, be kind to yourself. It is ok if you don't understand everything for the first one week. It is a new environment, and it is going to take time. Secondly, this means that you must be proactive and set yourself for success in your new job, no matter how hard it could be.

Here are some strategies to be successful in your dream job:

Strategy 1: Get Back to Your 90-day Plan

Remember the awesome 90-day plan you used to ace your interview? Time to dust it off, and put it to use. The reason you created this was not only to get the dream job but also to use it as a guide to figure out what you need to do in the first 90 days at that job.

During your first week, you are going to be onboarded and meet your various team members, including your boss. In one of those meetings, let your boss know you are going to work according to the 90-day plan you had shared during the interview. Give them a copy of it again to refresh his/her memory. Your boss usually would acknowledge this and give you the go-ahead; if not, they would suggest things to add/edit in your 90-day plan.

After getting your boss's blessings, it is *go time*. Print out the 90-day plan and stick it on the wall of your cube. Do this to remind yourself of the different things you need to accomplish in the first 90 days. Start implementing and learning the things you said you were going to do. Keep your boss updated during your one-on-one meetings every week to let them know how you are progressing through your goals. Doing this gives visibility to your boss that you are proactive, focused, and on a mission to succeed. When your annual performance review comes around, this will also be great to speak of as you can show your progress and achievements.

Strategy 2: Make Results Visible

Your boss does your performance review, but everyone around you gives feedback to your boss as well. This is especially true if you have a peer-to-peer feedback system, where everyone gives feedback about everyone else. So, it is important to keep your whole team posted on your accomplishments, so that they know you are contributing to the team and making a positive impact.

Some ways to do this:

- When you do something that helps another person significantly, try to have it documented.

    - If the person emails you their appreciation, save those appreciation emails in a separate folder for future reference.
    - If you do not receive an email from them, send an email saying you are glad that the solution you tried help them out, and they will reply acknowledging your effort.
    - You can also ask the person to send an email about your achievement with your boss cc'ed or ask them to document your accomplishment in some place which is publicly visible.

- In your daily team meetings (like stand-ups), ensure you mention the things you did that helped the team. This helps to build credibility and trust, and your colleagues will start paying attention to your efforts.
- Before your one-on-one's with your boss, document all the things you have accomplished in the past couple of weeks and send that as part of the agenda item to discuss. This not only helps to go over your accomplishments with your boss but also helps as a reference point during performance reviews.

Things that are not documented are never recognized as being done. This is a fact when you work in the corporate world.

Strategy 3: Be a Giver

In the book *Give and Take*, Adam Grant discusses how the most successful people we know were givers and not takers. A giver is a person who helps others without expecting anything in return. They put others' interests ahead of their own. A taker will help you out in return for a favor. They have to take care of themselves first before helping others.

I was a taker when I initially started in the IT industry. Whenever I helped people, I expected something in return. If they did not reciprocate my help, I used to get hurt, develop anger toward them, and sometimes be vindictive. Only after a few years did I realize how helping others is the only way to progress through work and life. I felt ashamed for my previous actions and decided to make a change shortly after. Since that shift, I have gone out of my way to help others in need, not because I will get something in return but because we are human. Gratitude, generosity, and compassion are what makes us move forward.

If you're not making someone else's life better, then you're wasting your time. Your life will become better by making other lives better. —Will Smith

Apart from documenting your accomplishments and making others know how you are impacting the team, you naturally should be helping your colleagues. This is especially true when they are struggling with something and you have the skill set, time, and resources to help them out. Just by helping people, I have made so many long-lasting friendships. A by-product of that was I got so many other connections and opportunities that I would never have got if I hadn't helped people in the first place.

I am not religious, but I am spiritual. I believe the universe has a way of noticing our good deeds and giving back help when we most need it.

So help others so you can grow in the company and succeed at your job, but also because it's the right thing to do.

Strategy 4: Socialize with Your Team

When you join a new company, it is important to know people at the company to help you out in times of need. The best way to do this is to socialize with your team and try to get to know them on a personal level. Yes, I know what you may be saying: "Raj, you are an extrovert, and it is easy for you to talk to anyone, but I am an introvert and a private person. I do not feel comfortable doing this." I get it; I was once an introvert myself: super shy, reserved, and had a fear of rejection. If you are a private person, it is OK. Just start to observe people who are of similar wavelengths as you or have common interests, and see if you could talk to them. This is not something that must happen within a day. It is a gradual process. So, don't be too hard on yourself, and just take it one step at a time.

Once you know someone on a personal level, the way you work with them drastically changes. These folks would go to any extent to help you out, especially at times when you mess up big time, and you need someone to help you out. This will happen at some point in your job. These are the folks who are going to be your confidants and support you through difficult times. And that's a two-way street, as I mentioned in *strategy 3*, you'll want to help them out too.

There are many ways you can socialize with your team. Some of the approaches I have followed in the past are as follows:

- *Sharing Drinks*: I am a huge craft beer fan. At one point, I had 100+ beers in my basement bar. Every Friday evening, I encouraged my colleagues to join me for a beer or two, to get to know them better. More often than not, people are always willing to join you for good beer. If you don't drink, no worries; join in the fun with lemonade, mocktails, or really any other beverage!
- *Sharing Food*: Volunteer to organize a potluck within your team. This is where each person makes a dish and shares it with the entire team. There is no better way to get into people's hearts than food. Trust me on this. It is a universal language that everyone understands, and it may also be a good way to share something from your culture (or at least a favorite recipe).
- *Sharing an Experience*: If you are in a leadership role, take your team to a sporting event: bowling or any other place where the team is forced to mingle with each other. This is a great way to get to know your team members on a personal level.

Strategy 5: Befriend Your Boss

Your boss is the most important resource for you when you join the company. I've been lucky to have great bosses throughout my career. In most cases, your manager is your boss. Occasionally, I have seen a lead engineer, a tech architect, or someone senior and more experienced in teams having direct reports. Whatever the case may be, it is really important to stay on the good side of your boss because at the end of the year he/she is going to help you get a salary increase or the promotion you always wanted as a reward for your hard work.

One way to do this is to get to know your boss on a personal level. During your one-on-one conversations, apart from just talking business, ask how their family is doing or share the news of any great event that happened in your life to open up the channel for more personalized conversations. Periodically, make it a point to ask them how they are doing because after all, they are human beings as well, and we need to recognize that.

Also, acknowledge anything good your boss does for you. Sometimes it's all about giving a word of appreciation, and a lot of managers may not get positive feedback or acknowledgment from those they manage. A few kind words or a short email can go a long way. When you appreciate their good deeds and efforts, they feel important and want to help you out even more. Finally, have open conversations with your boss. They need to know if their actions are affecting either you or the team. Most of the great bosses I worked for appreciated open and honest feedback. Just like you, they want to improve and do well in their jobs.

Strategy 6: Do the Tasks No One Else Wants to Do

When trying to be successful at your new job, you should be willing to do the tasks that no one else wants to do. You can get name recognition by doing this since people remember it. Many times, these are the tasks that make a big impact on teams, and your work could live on forever. (Talk about a legacy!)

For example, in one of the companies I worked for, teams were wasting a lot of time using Excel sheets to document certain information about the project, based on a new process that was mandated by the company. For months, teams were complaining about how time-consuming it was to enter details about the project on a daily basis in this wretched Excel sheet. Everyone wished there was a better solution for this, and they were looking for someone to fix this problem.

I noticed this pain-point the entire company was facing and volunteered to do something about it. I built a utility that automatically imported and exported information to and from the Excel sheet and filled in the required information automatically. This saved a considerable amount of time for teams. At that time, I did not realize the impact of my work.

But after several years, when I got in touch with my colleagues in that company, I heard people were still using the utility I built for the Excel sheet and remember me. In fact, they are still using it at the time of writing this book. This is the impact you can create when you volunteer to do the shitty things no one else wants to do. It is a great way to get your name on the top performer list.

SUMMARY OF CHAPTER 3

Six strategies to be successful at your dream job

- Strategy 1: Bring Back Your 90-day Plan

  - Get the 90-day plan approved by your boss, and get to work.

- Strategy 2: Make Results visible

  - Keep the whole team posted on your accomplishments.

- Strategy 3: Be a Giver

  - Help people be successful.

- Strategy 4: Socialize with Your Team

  - Get to know your team on a personal level.

- Strategy 5: Befriend Your Boss

  - Get to know your boss on a personal level.

- Strategy 6: Do the Tasks No One Else Wants to Do

- Volunteer to complete tasks that people think are not interesting or are time-consuming to do. People remember you when you do this.

CHAPTER 4
Becoming a Rockstar

· · · · · · · · · · · · · · · · · ·

*Ordinary is easy, but being extraordinary takes effort to
stand out of the crowd. You need to go the extra mile.*
—Unknown

Going the Extra Mile

Until now, we have covered different strategies to find your dream
job and be successful once you've landed it. But there is no fun in
being just ordinary? You need to set yourself miles apart from the
competition by being extraordinary. When people give you a task, they
need to realize that your work is always outstanding, and you always
go the extra mile.

For example, I started going to this old-school barbershop several
months ago. Ron, the sole owner and the barber, still has a barber's pole,
neon signs, the old school chairs, and the old cash register that you tap
on the side, and it opens up a drawer filled with change. The walls are
filled with Chicago sports memorabilia, and to top it all off, he uses an
old-school razor and shaving blade to finish off the haircut, followed
by a hot towel. Just the way they used to do it in the good old days.

I happened to stop by there once because my fancier hair salon
was closed. I'm so glad I did though, because it was a great learning
experience for me. At first, I was skeptical in terms of the quality of
service and the haircut I was going to get. Then, I started noticing
what makes Ron different from so many other people who have cut

my hair. It is not just that he charges less, but he gets outrageous tips because of his customer service. The minute you walk into his shop, he welcomes you with a smile. He offers coffee and beer for free. He reminds us to make ourselves comfortable. He remembers the names of my family members from my last visit and inquires about them. He also knows what my interests are. For example, for me, they are beer, sports, and technology; so, he strikes up a conversation related to these three topics. All of these details make me feel special and valued, and the crazy part is that even if my haircut is not the best of haircuts, this whole experience makes me want to go there again (but to be clear, the haircut is excellent as well). Most of his customers have been going to him for over 50 years, and he has had the shop for about 70 years. He is an outlier, overperformer, and a rockstar.

I'm sharing this story because sometimes it is the little things you do apart from your actual task that makes the difference. This is what I call the *maestro effect*. It is all about going to great lengths to provide value and making an impact on your life and others. When I entered the corporate world about 15 years ago, I started noticing that there were a handful of people who were always loved by my colleagues and had an outstanding reputation. Once I closely observed them, it was not their work that was outstanding but the little things they did in addition to what was expected from them that made the difference. They had the *maestro effect*. Since then, I have been following the strategy. The *maestro effect* made me get great performance reviews and consistently elevated me to rockstar status in most companies I worked for.

So what are the different things people do to stand out from the crowd? Below are some strategies which I have personally followed in my life and encouraged others to follow which made them a rockstar:

Six Strategies to Become a Rockstar

Strategy 1: Start Building Your Brand

Ordinary is easy, but being extraordinary is hard. When you continuously strive for greatness, after a while, it becomes a part of who you are. One key factor to get you in this path of awesomeness is building your brand.

What do I mean by building your brand? For example, say you have your favorite bodywash. You have been buying only that one brand of bodywash for several years. This is because you may like their advertisements, the ingredients, the fragrance, the price, the color of the packaging, the different sizes it is available in, and other factors that make you buy it regularly. Our personal brand is the same way. People get to know you not only because of your job description and name but also because of other skill sets such as communication, collaboration, teamwork, programming, out-of-the-box thinking, punctuality, empathy, and much more. Now, do you see the similarities with any particular brand? There are multiple factors that make up who you are and what you bring to the table. So how do you start building your brand?

- Do the Mind Dump exercise and identify your buckets.
- Identify different tasks you need to do under each bucket.
- Look at these tasks, and identify different things you need to do to accomplish your goals.
- While accomplishing your goals always figure out how you can add extra value to the work you do, and how it is impacting you and other people.

This is the first step in growing your brand, and making people recognize your skill set.

For example, apart from being an influencer in the software community, I am also a speaker, writer, tech career coach, volunteer, and craft beer and sports enthusiast. All these together make up my brand.

Strategy 2: Grow Your Network

Growing your network is crucial for your growth. You'll be surprised by the number of ideas and opportunities you get when you meet other people. For example, I would not have become a speaker or tech career coach if I had not met people outside my friend circle, who then gave me tips and inspiration to try out different things. Even my last three jobs were discovered through my connections.

The most successful people I know are usually great networkers who develop new relationships easily, and this eventually helps them when the need arises. Here are a couple of ways you can grow your network:

- Attend conferences, meetups, and other networking events. Make sure to meet new people and exchange business cards. After the exchange, quickly note down some hints at the back of the business card to remember the person later.
- Social media is a great way to connect with influencers. LinkedIn and Twitter are great for professional networking. Instagram and Facebook have entrepreneurs and other influencers in various other fields like photography, podcasts, parenthood and much more.
- Start engaging in online communities by sharing your ideas and commenting on other people's ideas and thoughts.
- Networking also is done within your circle. Try to get to know your colleagues and go out with them for lunch and dinners. They may have other friends who could be valuable in your network.

Strategy 3: Undersell and Overperform

An important concept in being successful is to undersell and overperform. How would you feel if you took your car in for an oil change, and you got the car back not only on time but your car was also completely detailed and washed? Wouldn't you be pleasantly surprised and remember that gesture? The same applies to your work life as well. Always commit to something you can definitely deliver, and when you complete the tasks, do something extra so that people will remember your work. This could be finishing the task way ahead of schedule, completing more tasks than you committed to, and other ways of going the extra mile to make your work stand out from others.

I do this by following a simple strategy: for any given task, identify the sub-tasks to complete first before accomplishing the main task, figure out the timeline you need to finish it on, add some buffer time on top of the normal timeline when committing to it, and lastly, once the main task is completed, think of anything extra that could be added to make the work stand out from others.

This strategy can be applied to leadership, sales, project management, and any other profession you are working in.

Strategy 4: Become an Effective Leader

I have seen two types of people in the IT industry—one who wants to get into leadership roles, and the other who wants to focus on their specialized skills and be an individual contributor. Both paths are good in their own ways. My experience is of transitioning from an individual contributor to leadership roles, so I want to share some strategies to become a leader.

Say you joined a company and got an opportunity to lead a team. What are the different things you need to do to become someone who could be a role model for others to follow? How do you become a rockstar leader? After speaking to other successful leaders and seeing them in action, I found that there are five necessary traits to be an efficient leader. My 15 years of learning, research, and experience in leadership all boils down to the following key factors:

1. Clarity in goals and objectives

The expectations of the team need to be communicated by the leader. It is hard to know in which direction to proceed without knowing the destination. Similarly, teams can't work toward a common goal if they do not understand what has to be accomplished within a given time frame.

The leader is responsible for ensuring that all team members are aware of their expectations and have sufficient know-how to meet the identified goals.

2. Effective communication

The leader needs to set standards and processes to increase communication between teams. This becomes especially important when working with distributed teams and is a core determinant of success in agile teams. There are different ways this can be achieved:

Truly follow agile practices (for IT teams)

It is crucial to ensure that teams follow the different agile practices set forth by the organization. Daily stand-ups, retrospective meetings, and planning meetings are common practices that occur in any agile methodology and should be respected. It's often necessary to give reminders and place emphasis on the value of these practices. As a leader, these messages must come from you.

Invest in collaboration tools

We need to break down barriers in communication in order to build highly collaborative teams. As part of this effort, identify and grant access to effective collaboration tools that teams can use easily. There are numerous video-conferencing and chat tools that enable people to have uninterrupted conversations with one another from anywhere. Evaluate tools to determine which makes sense for the team, and invest in the tool as soon as possible.

Encourage socialization

Apart from team members having constant communication related to work items, there also needs to be a channel through which they can get to know one another at a personal level. This helps bring teams closer and build lasting relationships. As a leader, enable this transition by hosting social events for both on-site and off-site employees. Show value to your off-site employees by bringing them together with the on-site employees regularly, to encourage even more team-building.

3.   Empower the team

Teams are more motivated when they are assigned clear responsibilities and are given ownership of tasks. Each individual on the team has a different skill set, and to increase productivity and team morale, the assigned responsibilities need to align with each person's strengths.

It is your responsibility as a leader to build a conducive environment for learning and empowered teams. There are many ways to do this, including the following:

Individual conversations

Use one-on-one conversations to identify individuals' strengths and interests. Assign tasks based on their strengths, and make sure they acknowledge accountability for these tasks. Have team members share their progress in team meetings to help them realize how their work matters to the project.

Rotating responsibilities

A great way to help individuals figure out their interests and passions is to rotate the various responsibilities within the team. For example, for each sprint, you could rotate the role of the Scrum Master so that each person gets a chance to experience the role. The same can be done with lead roles in software development and testing: one person would inherit the role of a lead and run point on all developer- or testing-related activities for that sprint.

This allows firsthand experience in different roles on agile teams, gives the feeling of empowerment and ownership, and helps to build self-organizing teams.

Peer coaching

As mentioned earlier, each team member has specific skills to offer. The first step to building highly motivated and cross-functional teams is to give sufficient training.

One way to do this is via peer coaching, where people are assigned mentors within the team to learn different skill sets. This helps people increase communication, learn new skills, gain insights into each other's work, and understand how their work impacts the project.

4. Proficiency at giving feedback

Receiving feedback on completed work is critical for the success of both an individual and the overall project. As a leader, it is your job to establish effective feedback loops to let team members know how they are performing and contributing to the company's overall goals. Feedback also helps team members understand areas that need improvement and take corrective actions promptly. You can't improve if you don't know how you're doing.

The feedback loops can be in the form of weekly or biweekly one-on-ones, retrospective meetings, daily stand-ups, planning meetings, and all-hands meetings with the entire group. Each meeting should address how the company or project is performing, how each individual has contributed, and the areas that still need improvement.

5.   Increase visibility

Everyone's work needs to be visible to ensure they are progressing according to plan and that they understand how their contributions impact the project. Various tools and dashboards can help people visualize their efforts and hold each other accountable for their actions. Most importantly, visibility gives the feeling of empowerment and ownership.

By adopting these practices, you can become a respected leader who builds high-performing, highly-collaborative teams.

Strategy 5: Take Control of Uncomfortable Situations

In every career, it is inevitable that someday you will be in an uncomfortable situation that will push you out of your comfort zone. This could happen in meetings in front of everyone or in a one-on-one interaction. Regardless of the circumstance, it is best to be prepared.

Early in my career, I had fears of both speaking and rejection. So, when I was faced with uncomfortable situations at work, I would let my fear dictate my decision and actions. I committed to tasks or events I didn't intend to and ended up feeling overworked and stressed. It happened so many times that I lost track. Once I realized I had to change this behavior, I started noticing how masterful communicators got out of similar situations unharmed. Based on that, I identified three strategies that can help you get control of any situation:

1.   Handling Spotlight Situations

Have you been in meetings where you are put on the spot and asked to explain something or to commit to a task you don't want to do? These situations happen regularly in the corporate world. It is a curveball that hits you when you least expect it. After failing numerous times to handle these kinds of situations, I finally discovered two tried-and-tested strategies that always work no matter who you are or what kind of situation you are boxed into:

Ask Clarifying Questions

When someone puts you on the spot and asks you to explain or commit to something, first pause and take a deep breath. Our gut reaction is to reply immediately, but do not do that. Force yourself not to answer immediately. Yes, it is hard, but with practice, it becomes a habit.

Secondly, try to ask a clarifying question to buy yourself more time. The questions could be as follows:

- Could you please repeat that one more time?
- Were you asking me about issue x or issue y?
- Is this a higher priority task than the one I am working on?
- Is this related to the current project we are working on?
- Or is there a deadline associated with this task?

The point is to ask a question to get more ideas on what is being asked from you. A lot of people are scared to do this, but trust me, it is better than answering something immediately and looking like a fool. I have been there and done that.

Follow the "I Will Get Back to You" Strategy

Another way to prevent yourself from getting trapped into doing something is to follow the "I will get back to you" strategy. When someone puts you on the spot and asks you something, if you are unfamiliar with the questions or unclear on the answer, just say "let me get back to you on that." Not everyone knows everything at any given situation, so it is ok to buy more time by saying you are going to check on the answer or do more research. People understand you are human and are usually satisfied with this reply. For more accountability, you may want to add a timeframe, saying "I will get back to you by the end of the day" or "I can circle back to you by tomorrow at noon." Also, if you want to sound a bit more confident, give them two options, both of which work for you, such as "I can get back to you Wednesday afternoon, or would you rather tomorrow afternoon?" This way they have two options, both of which are to have you reach out to them at a later time.

Some ways to use this strategy include the following:

- I do not remember the answer to that, but let me get back to you after this meeting.
- I am not sure whether I can make a decision right now without looking at my notes and getting more context. Why don't I get back to you on that after this call?
- I have to look into my priorities offline and will let you know.
- I am pretty sure we used this approach to solve that problem; let me get back to you on this and give you a confirmation.

2.   Power of Safety Language

Say you have two weather apps that tell you the daily weather forecast:

App 1:

The weather app says the chances of rain are 100 percent. You notice this, so you dress up appropriately, wearing your raincoat and boots and putting your stuff in a waterproof bag. Then you step out of the house. You notice that it is sunny and hot, and people are wearing their tank tops, t-shirts, and shorts. You are the odd man out, and you feel stupid for being overdressed.

App 2:

The weather app says the chances of rain are 30 percent. You notice this, so you just want to be prepared. You dress up in water-resistant clothes which are comfortable, wear comfy shoes which you can afford to get wet since they wash easily, grab an umbrella and step out of the house. You notice that it is sunny and hot, and people are wearing their tank tops, t-shirts, and shorts. You do not feel that out of place as you are still wearing comfortable clothes and did not go overboard by preparing for a monsoon rain.

Which weather app would you trust the next time for weather updates? App 1 or App 2?

When I posed this question to my followers, they unanimously said *App 2*, and I would have chosen the same.

Let's take this example and apply it to your work environment. Have you ever been in any of these situations?

- You are working on one task, and suddenly, your manager passes by and asks you to do a different task. Since you were caught by surprise, you immediately say YES even without thinking about all the other things you have to finish that day.
- You are put on the spot in a meeting and "voluntold" (told to volunteer) for a task. To avoid any embarrassment, you immediately say YES, without even thinking. You finally find that it was a shitty task no one wanted to do, but you got assigned to it already.
- Your colleague asks you to complete his/her task since they are too busy, and you say YES just because you want to be projected as being nice to them, without realizing that you already have tasks piled up for yourself, which need attention first.
- You are in a meeting and asked to agree to some decision, and you agree because of peer pressure. (This is also known as "group think.")

This is where "safety language" helps. It is an approach where you commit to something without committing, or you acknowledge something but buy time to commit. These are situations where you may use the following phrases:

1. "It appears to be a picture of…"
2. "It might fail under these circumstances"
3. "It appears to fail"
4. "You may be right"
5. "I might disagree with that"
6. "I've noticed that…"
7. "My experience has been…"

You use words like could, may be, might not, may, etc.

So the next time a manager approaches you with a task which he/she thinks is important, you can take a deep breath and say, "Hi, I would love to work on that task, but COULD I DO that after I complete this one?" Or the next time you are asked to agree on something but you do not want to, you could say "I agree with four out of the five points, but I might disagree with this point due to these reasons."

Safety language is a powerful approach to focus on higher priority tasks, avoid distractions, free yourself from peer pressure, and prevent yourself from painting yourself into a corner because of overcommitting to things or not having the flexibility to change your decision.

So, remember when you are asked something or in an uncertain situation, pause, take a deep breath, and use safety language.

Strategy 6: Switch Jobs Internally

We work hard to get the dream job we always wanted. Several months or years into our position, we slowly start discovering other opportunities, and we may realize our true passion is in another role and not in the current one. Remember, I said that discovering our dream job is an iterative process? Your interests may keep changing as you get exposed to more and different responsibilities, technologies, and job types.

Once we make this discovery, a gut reaction is to start looking for a job outside our current organization immediately. But we fail to realize that the job we are looking for may exist within the company itself, and it's possible to switch roles internally. If you love the company you work for, then this option works best for you. There is no need for relocation or any change in your normal life. You come to the office as usual but do another job instead of your original one.

Also, in one of the companies I worked for, they had a great program called the "shadow program." Instead of completely changing your job, you get an opportunity to shadow a person who already works in the job you are interested in, so you can figure out if it meets your interests and expectations. This helps to get a taste of your new job without having to fully transition into it.

SUMMARY OF CHAPTER 4

Six strategies to become a rockstar

- Strategy 1: Start Building Your Brand

    - Your brand is the single most important component to grow in your career.

- Strategy 2: Grow Your Network

    - Attend networking events, use the power of social media, and engage with online communities.

- Strategy 3: Undersell and Overperform

    - Commit on performing tasks within a given timeline, and deliver well ahead of the set timeline.

- Strategy 4: Become an Effective Leader

    - Follow the five traits—clarity in goals and objectives, effective communication, empower teams, give effective feedbacks, and increase visibility—to become a leader whom everyone wants to follow.

- Strategy 5: Take control of uncomfortable situations

- When put on the spot or forced into uncomfortable situations, use these three strategies: safety language, ask clarifying questions, and "will get back to you" strategy. It will get you out of it without embarrassment.

- Strategy 6: Switch Jobs Internally

  - When you realize you may be interested in a new role, remember you can always switch to another one within the company, and still be successful in it.

CHAPTER 5
Unleashing Your Power and Igniting Exponential Growth

· ·

You can waste your lives drawing lines. Or you
can live your life crossing them.

—Shonda Rhimes

Start Your Journey of Self-Exploration

You found your dream job, and you are successful in it. You have applied all the strategies you have learned from the previous chapters, and you are loving life. But, if you are reading this book, it means that you were meant to do more than just being successful at your job. You want to explore the other opportunities life gives you, and you want to find the true meaning and purpose in your life.

In 2017, I had a great job. I was leading a team of highly smart and successful people. I was doing some really cool stuff related to technology and my team. I was still getting great performance reviews, bonuses, salary raises, and I could not complain. But that June, I slowly started realizing that, for about a decade, I had been constantly working hard, putting in the effort to be successful, and had the notoriety and salary I needed, but, I felt there was something missing. My work was not giving me any meaning or purpose in life. It felt like I was in the movie *Groundhog Day*, where I was doing the same thing over and over again, without making a significant impact on others.

So, I started a journey of exploration for the next four months, consuming copious amounts of information through reading books, listening to podcasts, and interviewing various people to figure out what makes them happy and how they discover something meaningful. In four months, I read over 20 books and listened to about 150 podcasts related to leadership, productivity, mindfulness, self-improvement, nutrition, and communication (all while working and house-hunting with my wife!). I read various biographies to get inspiration and was trying to figure out my purpose in life. I wanted to make an impact not only in my life but in others' as well.

It was during this time that I started my company: ChaiLatte Consulting. My wife and I decided on this name as it represented who we are and what we stand for. We support diversity, inclusion, and equality. And my wife is American (of European descent), and I am Indian. So, ChailLatte was the perfect name. We now have a true embodiment of this term—a beautiful infant son.

This journey of self-discovery made me realize that I was chasing the wrong dream. I thought fame and money were everything, but making an impact in other people's lives was what ultimately mattered. This is what gives you meaning and purpose in life.

Since I started my company, I have learned various lessons that have helped me discover new strengths and grow as an individual. Following these approaches will help you get more focus in life and lead to exponential personal growth.

Ten Strategies for Exponential Growth

Strategy 1: Power of Morning Routines

What is the one thing common between Tim Cook, Warren Buffet, Richard Branson, Jeff Bezos, Oprah Winfrey? They all have morning routines. They have been doing the same set of tasks for decades that set their day up for productivity, focus, and success. These tasks may include reading, meditation, journaling, morning coffee, drinking water or smoothies, exercising, planning tasks, or many others. But on a high level, it involves carving out time to nourish the mind, body, and soul.

I started experimenting with morning routines in 2016 but was never consistent. I tried journaling, exercising, meditation, drinking water and smoothies, and reading—one at a time or a combination of them at once. But, after a lot of trial and error, I finally figured out the ideal morning routine that sets me up for a successful day. This is how my routine looks like:

- Wake up around 5:30 a.m.
- Turn on the coffee pot which I prep with coffee and water the previous night.
- Stretch for a few minutes.
- Brush my teeth, and skim through my email for about five minutes.
- Drink 12 oz. glass of water.
- Meditate for 10 minutes.
- Pour my coffee, and take my first sip.
- Peruse the different tasks that need to be completed that particular day. Prioritize them, and decide which are my top three tasks for the day that must be completed.
- Turn on symphony or any instrumental music I have already saved in my playlist.
- Work on a creative task that usually falls under the category of "content creation" like videos, blogs, articles, and anything that would need critical thinking and focus.

I have followed this routine for about two years, and it has done wonders for my life.

Remember, you are not going to nail a morning routine on your first try. You need to experiment with things for a period of time and analyze what is working and what isn't.

EXERCISE

1. Take a paper and a pen. List different things you like doing that makes you calm, relaxed, and focused.
2. Pick one item from the list.
3. Do it every morning for a week.
4. Next week, pick another item from the list.
5. In the second week, continue doing the item you started to do in the first week, and implement the second item along with it.
6. Continue this routine in the morning for the next two weeks such that you have started doing four items in a month.
7. Analyze which ones you like doing, and which ones are not effective.
8. Eliminate the ones that are not effective, and add the next item on your original list from step 1.
9. Repeat this the next month.

Strategy 2: Nourish Your Body With Exercise

I am grateful that I have a well-functioning body. I have arms, legs, vision, and everything I need for anything I want to do. I admire those who are able to persevere through physical limitations. They are far more resilient than I am, and they have worked hard even when things weren't easy, especially by respecting and pushing their bodies. They want to do the best they can with what they were born with. Most of us do not realize how lucky we are to have everything in our body, and unfortunately, we treat our body like shit.

I grew up my entire life as a fat kid. I was ridiculed for my appearance and weight by my own family and friends. This made me develop severe body image issues, and I let others' opinions define who I was. I was tired of living such a life and wanted to make a change.

After having my shorts rip right in half the day after my wedding, and then another pair, four weeks later, I started realizing how different my body had become (and how the shorts remained the same size). On January 1st, 2016, I decided to change my physical life and lost 50 pounds in six months by joining a wellness group, playing basketball, and running. I read books on nutrition and found out that a lot of things I thought were healthy were really garbage for my body. Since then, I have maintained my weight under any circumstance—even when traveling, having a newborn, sleeping less than five hours a day, being in the midst of a pandemic, and even when I am physically hurt. Yes, even when I am injured, I try to do some sort of workout to be consistent. For example, in 2017, I broke my right hand while playing basketball. I could not use it for over three months. For the first couple of weeks, I was depressed and wondered why this had happened to me. Then, I got motivation from some of my friends who were born with disabilities, and I started climbing the stairs in my apartment, which had close to 40 floors, to get my cardio exercise. This is what being persistent is—finding a way to get stuff done even when there are obstacles.

Once you start forcing yourself to take action on becoming healthy and staying consistent, respecting your body through exercise and good nutrition becomes a habit. This being said, by no means I am perfect. I still struggle with using food as a coping mechanism when I am stressed, but at least, I make sure I work out, and I am so grateful for my body.

As a result of taking care of your body, you have more energy, lower stress levels and anxiety, are more productive at your work, come up with bigger and better ideas, have laser focus on different tasks you perform, and actually start enjoying your time with family, knowing you are focusing on your health not only for yourself but for your family as well.

Strategy 3: Do Meditation

For several years, I suffered from severe anxiety, depression, and panic attacks. I was prescribed medication by a therapist, but it made me tired, apathetic, and gain weight. In 2016, I was tired of living such a life and started looking for alternative solutions to get back mental and physical stability. That is when I stumbled upon meditation, with encouragement from my therapist.

I am a very skeptical person, so I thought meditation was voodoo stuff. Then a friend of mine recommended the Headspace app (you have other similar apps like Calm, Aura, and many more). I started using this app and loved how they have different meditation packs (a series of exercises) for anxiety, depression, happiness, and other feelings I was experiencing at that time. Each of these exercises could be customized for 5, 10, 15, or 20 minutes. So, I gave this a try.

Three months after starting meditation, I was able to gain mental peace, control, and focus, so I worked with my doctors and stopped my medications, and have been medication-free since mid-2016. Doing meditation made me more mindful of the different things around me. I started paying attention to small acts of generosity and kindness and developed an appreciation for having all the things I need to live a life with meaning and purpose. My stress levels and anxiety reduced drastically, and I started viewing the world with a different lens—the lens of gratitude and forgiveness.

I believe in the power of meditation—the way it can help individuals navigate struggles and become calmer and happier so they are able to start loving life again.

Strategy 4: Do Deep Work

In today's multitasking-centric world, we try to work on different tasks at the same time and end up not completing or focusing on anything. We do not give our 100 percent effort in the tasks we do because of constant distractions. You have messages on Slack, phones, and Facebook; emails (which seem to multiply like rabbits if you ignore them for any period of time); or even your coworkers interrupting you while you're doing important tasks, because you are physically visible in the workplace or they just want to say hi.

Some startling research about these constant distractions:

- It takes up to 23 minutes to regain concentration after interruption[4].
- On average, we check our emails 30 times per hour[5].
- On average, people spend four hours a day on their smartphones.[6] This is the same as half a full-time job!

So, this is the world we live in. Do you want to be sucked into these distractions? Or make a change to do focused work?

Four years ago, I decided to follow the latter approach. I read *Deep Work* by Cal Newport, and it changed my life. Since then, I have been practicing deep work, and it has dramatically improved the quality of my work. The basic concept of deep work is to have focused time blocks for specific focused work. Before your workday ends, spend 15 minutes to prioritize and plan out the next day's work. One interesting concept discussed in the book was to practice *productive meditation*.

---

[4]   "It Takes 23 Minutes to Recover From a Distraction at Work…" 4 May. 2017, https://www.inc.com/nicholas-mcgill/it-takes-23-minutes-to-recover-from-a-distraction-at-work-heres-how-to-minimize-.html.

[5]   "How much time are you spending on email?—The Front Blog." 20 Jul. 2018, https://frontapp.com/blog/how-much-time-are-you-spending-on-email.

[6]   "Are You On Your Phone Too Much? The Average Person…" 30 Oct. 2018, https://www.inc.com/melanie-curtin/are-you-on-your-phone-too-much-average-person-spends-this-many-hours-on-it-every-day.html.

This is a period where you are occupied physically by doing activities like walking, jogging, or driving while concentrating on a problem. You spend time thinking about it and try to find a solution for it, but you're not concentrating on only that, so your brain is able to look at the puzzle pieces differently. I do this on my runs, and this is yet another reason for me to exercise. Finally, be rigorous about the time you spend on productive versus unproductive tasks, and one great way to do this is to track your time. I use Toggl for time tracking, and it makes my life so much easier. My wife works on billable projects, so she needs to have everything broken into 15-minute increments. For the last five years, she's been using an Excel sheet she created with formulas and color-coding to track her time. You should do whatever works for you so you can see where your time is going; is it more social networking than business networking?

One of the ways I have adapted the concepts of *Deep Work* in my life is to block my calendar with different tasks that need to be accomplished during the week. I have 1-hour time blocks throughout the day. Each time block in the calendar has the name of the task I need to work on, and I use the notes section to add any description of things that could help me accomplish that task. I create up to 4–5 time blocks per day.

For example, if I have to write an article for a magazine, I will have two 1-hour time blocks during the day, with the name of the task on the calendar as "Write Tech Magazine Article." Under this calendar meeting/time block, I fill the notes sections with details of what I need to accomplish the task, like the title of the article, an outline of what I am going to write, websites I am going to use for research, etc. In this way, I do not have to think about what I need to do when I have free time. Everything has already been scheduled on the calendar, and I just need to work. This is like school, where you have classes and descriptions already on your calendar, and you just show up at that time and do the work.

Remember, *time is money*, protect it!

Strategy 5: Focusing and De-focusing

How many of you have had this situation before where you work the entire day on multiple tasks without breaks, and you are still barely able to keep up with them? At the end of the day, you feel like you were hit by a tsunami; you are brain-dead and tired. And maybe you haven't even accomplished anything concrete! If this is a regular occurrence in your life, then you are not alone.

The current industry is geared toward accomplishing as many tasks as possible in a workweek consisting of at least 40 hours. Companies believe longer work hours is what makes employees more valuable. This is far from the truth and is a counterintuitive approach to working efficiently.

Various research studies have found that the human mind can focus only for 50–90 minutes at a stretch.[7] After which, a 10–20 minutes break is necessary to recharge the brain. So, we need to take frequent breaks throughout the day to be more productive at work.

I usually do 1-hour focused work on a particular task and then take a 10-minute break. During the break, I get out of my home office, drink a glass of water, read a page from a book, or do twenty push-ups to recharge my brain. You could do the same even at a physical office by going for a walk around the office building, walking the stairs for a couple of floors, or refilling your beverage of choice at the break room.

By learning to focus and de-focus, you can be highly productive and do your best work.

---

7   "Brief diversions vastly improve focus, researchers find…" 8 Feb. 2011, https://www.sciencedaily.com/releases/2011/02/110208131529.htm.

EXERCISE

1. Schedule two 10-minute breaks on the calendar: one in the morning and another in the afternoon.

2. Set a 30-minute lunch break, and physically get away from your desk to another location.

3. During these breaks take a quick walk, stretch, read a book, listen to a podcast, or do something that relaxes you and isn't work.

Strategy 6: Planning Daily/Weekly Tasks

One of the most overlooked life skills is self-management because we often talk about time management. But, it's a misnomer—you cannot manage time. Time goes on whether we like it or not. We need to manage the way we work and prioritize tasks at a given time. Not everything is important.

The most successful people manage their tasks with the same level of commitment and seriousness as closing multi-million dollar deals. They know if they start focusing on the lower-priority items, they are going to miss out on bigger opportunities by not focusing on the higher-priority ones.

This is why planning your daily and weekly tasks is crucial to exponential growth. After talking to numerous successful people and a lot of trial and error in my personal life, I finally figured out a plan to manage my tasks. It has made me substantially more productive, and I have recommended it to vice presidents, CTOs, and directors, who have all found success with this skill.

This is how it works:

Daily Task Planning

- Each morning, spend just 5–10 minutes reviewing which tasks need to be accomplished for the day with the help of a to-do list.

- Prioritize the list by giving each task a number from 1 to 10. My rule is to finish the top three items on my list every day. Any remaining unfinished tasks get carried over to the next day.
- Schedule blocks of uninterrupted time, each focusing on one particular task. I usually try to do 4–5 blocks per day (about 1-hour each as mentioned in *strategy 4*).
- At the end of the day, spend five minutes to review what tasks were accomplished and what gets carried over to the next day.

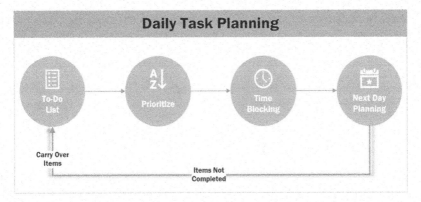

Download the Daily Task Planning workflow image here: www. skyrocketyourcareerbook.com/resources.

Weekly Task Planning

As part of my job, I have five categories I focus on: learning, reading, content creation, career coaching, and speaking. I want to make sure I dedicate time to each one of them. As I previously mentioned, I track my time using an app called Toggl. So, I am able to analyze how much time I spend on each of these tasks. Based on this information, I created a budget for my time, with each block being 1-hour.

- 2 time blocks per week for learning and reading-related tasks
- 4 time blocks for content creation
- 8 time blocks for career coaching
- The remainder is for speaking

I usually keep Monday, Tuesday, and Wednesday as my "meeting" days and reserve Thursday and Friday for tasks that need my creativity and thinking.

These time blocks are not set in stone, and they often vary based on my week. But, I have a general idea of the amount of effort I need to dedicate to tasks under each of these buckets.

Strategy 7: End-of-day Routines

There are people who are workaholics because they either enjoy their work or they think it will help them get a bigger salary or promotion. They end up working long hours, sacrificing time with family, friends, and personal care. The interesting part is that most of the work they do past 6 p.m. is non-essential work, which could be done the next day. They do it just because their mind is tuned to doing work, and that is the way it has always been.

I was someone who worked long hours and made assumptions that some of the work I was doing was important. Only later did I find out that half of the things I had done weren't urgent and sat in folders and email inboxes in the same state as I had left them for days, months, and even years without any further action.

I once was so burnt-out from work that I was admitted to the hospital. After that experience, I realized that life is too short, and I cannot let even a minute pass by without evaluating the priorities in my life. After I got discharged, I started asking myself *"Where in my life do I have the most stress?"*

Apparently, working long hours through the evening and nights was one of the biggest stressors for me. So, I came up with an end-of-day routine. Having such a routine helps to maintain sanity and helps to prioritize you as a person over your work. This is my routine:

- I finish work between 5–6 p.m.

- I look over my calendar for the next day to get an idea of what will be happening.
- I take five minutes to write down the things I need to accomplish the next day.
- Then I close my laptop, and turn off my monitor.
- I always have a family dinner with my wife and my son (and of course, I work on dinner if it's not ready when I'm done working).
- My wife and I get our son ready for bed with his own evening routine. (His involves bubble baths; mine, unfortunately, does not.)
- At 8 p.m., our son goes to sleep. After that, my wife and I talk about how our day went and catch up. Maybe even watch a TV show together.
- At 10 p.m., we get ready for bed.
- We read for at least five minutes in bed.
- We have a couple's "question-a-day" journal we fill in every night. It takes less than two minutes. We also have a small journal to document our son's life (major milestones like new foods or "firsts") that we write in occasionally.
- Then, before we go to sleep, we ask each other three questions every night without fail.

  - What is one thing you are grateful for today?
  - What is one thing you are happy about today?
  - What is one thing you could improve on today?

Yes, there are days when I have to put in a couple of hours of work at night to finish up something, or my wife may have to do her own work. But most days, we try to stick to the above schedule. We have been following this routine for the past couple of years, and it has immensely helped us prioritize family time over work.

Most successful people have end-of-day routines, as it gives structure in their life and mirrors the morning routine. Try to form yours.

EXERCISE

1. Identify what your regular work hours look like. Use Toggl to track your time for a couple of weeks.

2. Block your calendar after work hours to ensure that no one schedules you for meetings, and your mind gets trained to know work time is over.

3. Talk to your significant other about what you can do as a family every single weekday after work. Come up with a game plan.

4. Take 10 minutes to analyze what tasks were completed today, write down tasks that have to be done the next day, and look over the calendar for the next day to get a feel of how your day will look like.

5. Put your laptop on "Do Not Disturb" mode, close it, and turn off any monitors connected to it.

6. Spend time with family, and implement your game plan.

7. Before going to sleep, read for at least five minutes.

8. Ask your significant other the three questions listed above.

If you are single, it does not mean you cannot have end-of-day routines. You can just customize the above plan based on your schedule, interests, and lifestyle.

Strategy 8: Continuous Learning

There is a famous quote by Loyal 'Jack' Lewman: *Never stop learning; for when we stop learning, we stop growing.*

This is so true. Only when you continuously learn, do you discover new interests and opportunities.

Since 2011, I have put in the effort to purposely learn new things. I started seeking mentors who could help me in public speaking and getting out of my comfort zone. I read books on leadership, motivation, mindfulness, self-motivation, and productivity to both become a better leader and to gain control of my mental and physical health. I started taking online courses to teach myself new programming languages, and I built software utilities that helped many people in various companies I worked for. Finally, I worked with coaches to get my business up and running the right way, while continuing to learn from courses and my interviews with other successful entrepreneurs.

People around us (who are often jealous of our success) often tell us to only learn things that relate to our work. This is bullshit. If I had listened to these folks, I would have never tried various things like those I previously mentioned, and I would not be where I am today. In fact, you never know how something you learn from one field can be applied to another field.

For example, after Steve Jobs got fired from Apple, he took a calligraphy course. When he rejoined Apple as the CEO, he applied principles from this class, which helped build the beautifully designed keyboards of the MacBook which I am currently using to write this book.

So, if you don't believe me, at least take it from Steve Jobs; to be a rockstar, you need to keep learning.

Strategy 9: The Power of Delegation

To be a great leader and focus on things that matter, you need to start delegating. Unfortunately, I learned this late in the game; I was a control freak at the beginning of my IT career. If there was a task assigned to me but another person offered his/her help, I refused to accept it since I was scared they would screw things up. They would not do things *my way* or may get recognition for something that I should have got recognized for.

Once I started leading teams, I realized that one person cannot do everything. There is only so much time in a day. If you try working on everything, then nothing gets done completely, or some important things do not get our fullest attention. Now that I am an entrepreneur, it is even more important as I want to work on my business by making critical decisions and growing it, rather than doing all the admin work that is not strategic for my growth but is vital to keep the business running.

To delegate work and ensure it meets your expectations, follow these steps:

- Give clear instructions on when and how to accomplish the task.
- Be explicit on the expected outcome.
- Provide guidance when necessary.
- Monitor the progress behind the scenes, but do not micromanage.
- Give immediate feedback if you see something slipping.
- Delegate the right things to the right people.

Remember, once you start delegating, it frees up time to focus on more strategic and important tasks.

Strategy 10: Advanced LinkedIn Strategies

Remember in *chapter 1* I told you LinkedIn is the most overlooked, the most underrated, and yet the most powerful social media channel for professionals? Yes, it is. I am just re-confirming it, in case you forgot I told you so earlier.

Updating your LinkedIn profile is a continuous process. It is like doing an oil change for your vehicle; you have to do it periodically, and if you ignore it, the car does not work to its fullest potential (*and it eventually dies, as you may have already guessed*). Similarly, your LinkedIn profile keeps evolving and should be updated in a timely manner when you accomplish tasks, earn promotions, change jobs or positions, and take on new responsibilities. If it is not done regularly, then you lose future opportunities and can become irrelevant in a hot job market.

Apart from constant updates to your LinkedIn profile, there are other tricks to adopt to make you visible to people so you can get your next big opportunity. They are as follows:

Follow #Hashtags

Hashtags are one of the most important facets of any social media channel, including LinkedIn. People follow hashtags to receive information relevant to their interests in their news feed. Using hashtags will help you stay updated on the latest trends in your field and is also a way to discover what interesting work other people are doing. It gives you a chance to connect with new individuals and organizations who have similar interests, so you are both able to grow your networks and you can find your dream job.

Steps to follow hashtags on LinkedIn:

- Use LinkedIn search bar and search for a keyword with hashtags. For example, search for #careerdevelopment
- You will see different posts with this hashtag. Most importantly, at the top, you will see the number of people following this tag. Click on "Follow" (Tip: *Follow hashtags with more followers to get more posts and information, and connect with more people.*)

Follow Influencers

Similar to hashtags, you can follow people on LinkedIn who give you motivation, inspiration, and post great content. For example, if you want to follow Bill Gates, search his name just like what you did for hashtags, and click "Follow."

Improve Your Feed Option

This is a great option that people do not know about, and it can filter content to display what is most relevant to help you grow.

Click on the "…" on the top right section of any post on LinkedIn. Choose the option "Improve My Feed." LinkedIn will give you recommendations on different hashtags to follow and people to connect with, based on your profile, and will share LinkedIn usage patterns. Instead of being overwhelmed with irrelevant content, your feed will be based on your interests, so you are more easily able to connect with other like-minded people.

Comment, Share, and Post

People need to know you too are an influencer on LinkedIn. You want people to start following you instead of just Bill Gates. The simplest way to begin this process is to start commenting, sharing, and posting content relevant to your industry and skill sets. Through this, other people will discover you, and it gives you an opportunity to get more connections on LinkedIn.

While posting, make sure to tag those individuals and organizations using @ symbol to let them know you acknowledge their content and use relevant hashtags to make the post reach the right audience.

Use only a maximum of four hashtags as the LinkedIn algorithm sees only the first four hashtags in your post, and if you add more, it will de-prioritize your post. This means the post may not be visible to as many people as you would have liked. Again, at the time of the publication of this book, this is how the algorithm works. But they update their algorithms regularly, so this may change in the future.

EXERCISE

1. Follow five hashtags which have the most followers, based on your area of interest.
2. Follow five influencers who you respect and admire.
3. Use the "Improve my feed" option to customize your interests and connect with new people.
4. Like, Comment or Share one post on your news feed every day.

Do this regularly and people will start discovering you.

SUMMARY OF CHAPTER 5

Ten Strategies for Exponential Growth

- Strategy 1: Power of Morning Routines

  - Discover and follow a morning ritual to set your day up for success.

- Strategy 2: Nourish Your Body With Exercise

  - Take care of your body to boost performance at work and personal life.

- Strategy 3: Do Meditation

  - Use meditation as a tool for mental clarity, focus, and stability.

- Strategy 4: Practice Deep Work

  - Use uninterrupted, focused time to be highly productive and perform your best.

- Strategy 5: Focusing and De-focusing

  - Take breaks between tasks to recharge your brain.

- Strategy 6: Plan Daily/Weekly Tasks

  - Plan the tasks you will be working on ahead of time, and strategize your effort by spending more time on high-priority tasks.

- Strategy 7: End-of-Day Routines

  - Have a set end-of-day routine to train your body and mind that it is time to relax, unwind, and spend time for personal care and family.

- Strategy 8: Continuous Learning

  - Invest in yourself through continuous learning, even if it doesn't seem to relate to your current work.

- Strategy 9: The Power of Delegation

  - To be a great leader, you need to focus on the strategic high-priority tasks, and delegate other non-strategic tasks to other people.

- Strategy 10: Advanced LinkedIn Strategies

  - Regularly update your profile; follow hashtags and influencers; improve your feed options; and start sharing, liking, and commenting on posts.

CHAPTER 6
Conclusion

. . . .

The only thing worse than being blind is having sight but no vision.
—Helen Keller

Kids Teach Us Life Lessons

t is amazing what you can learn from your kids. Of course, when people would tell me this when I was single, with no plans of marriage or kids, I thought they were just bluffing. When my son was born, though, I saw for myself how children can teach you the life lesson that anything is possible.

Here is a simple example: One day, my son was trying to grab a toy, which was far from his reach. He was still not able to crawl, so he had to stretch and try to slide himself to different places, so I joked to my wife that he was going to take all day to grab the toy. We let him play by himself for twenty minutes or so, while we supervised from across the room.

What we noticed was that in those twenty minutes, he had grabbed the toy and of course, was putting it in his mouth like what babies do. I was pleasantly surprised as I thought there was no way he was going to grab with his "flailing turtle" movements, but he finally did.

This was a learning moment for me. Babies try so hard to talk, crawl, and walk. For example, they fall millions of times before they start walking. They do not say, "Screw this shit, walking is too hard. I am going to give up, lay here, and ask for help the rest of my life." When our babies and toddlers have this much resilience, why can't we model the same behavior?

Despite our kids looking to us as role models, we complain about life, we are lazy to perform our daily tasks (myself included sometimes), and we do not give our 100 percent to accomplish goals. We easily give up and tell ourselves, "That is ok. I will try it later," or even, "This is too hard, and I can't handle this anymore." What would my son think about me if I do not reflect the same behavior he does?

This is a gentle reminder for all of us that every day we need to strive for greatness; if not for us, at least for our children.

Elon Musk said, *If something is important enough, even if the odds are against you, you should still do it.*

Everything Starts with a Vision

Imagine yourself doing great, impactful things. In this visualization, you could be a leader everyone wants to follow, speaking in front of thousands of people and motivating them (which is my vision), doing work to help people suffering through poverty, lack of education, and giving them a second chance in life, or becoming the best parent you could be. Everyone has different dreams, which map to their visions. Vision focuses on what you ultimately want to become.

Start with your vision. Every day when you wake up, remind yourself why you are doing what you're doing. If what you are doing does not get you on the path to reaching your vision, then stop doing that, and figure out something else to do that could get you there. Identify goals to reach your vision, and identify tasks to reach these goals. This is how we all can keep marching forward to fulfill our dreams.

Everyone has a gift. We were born on this Earth to make a difference in our lives and others'. We have different talents, and it is up to us to discover our talents. Try to figure out what would make an impact in your life, and in the lives of others'. During this process, you will fail many times; sometimes it could be small, but other times it could be from a complete curveball you did not expect, which will sock you hard in your face, and knock you down really hard. But, as we learned before, we are resilient people who can get back on our feet. Learn from these experiences, and keep marching forward toward your goals.

When life gives you mountains, put those hiking shoes on and start hiking.
—Unknown

Be Kind to Yourself

The problem with us as humans is that the way we treat ourselves is different than the way we treat others. We are kind to our best friend, and make sure we treat him/her with respect. But, when we mess up or do something that we do not like, we berate ourselves. We tell ourselves we are not good enough, we always mess up, we are stupid, and we do not deserve a second chance. Would you say these things to your best friend? Of course, you wouldn't. Then, why do you treat yourself any differently?

By no means I am perfect. I too have those moments where I am upset with myself over different actions and circumstances, but I try hard to realize that to err is human. Only when we mess up, do we learn and grow, and it is through that growth that we become better people. The golden rule states "Treat others as you want to be treated." I would like to add to that, and say "treat yourself with respect first, and emulate that to others."

So, start noticing the positive things in life whenever you mess up. There is an opportunity for kindness and gratefulness in everything you do for yourself and others.

My Final Thoughts

The seed to write a book was first planted in my mind in 2016. I knew I had a story worth sharing, which could inspire other people going through journeys similar to mine. The book I had imagined publishing was a memoir highlighting my story as an immigrant in a foreign land, and how I converted adversities into opportunities. But in April 2020, my friend Monique Lindner mentioned she was going to write a book and was joining a writing group led by Gahmya Drummon-Bey (my awesome book writing coach). Monique asked me whether I would be interested to join the group. I was trying to juggle my full-time business, take care of my infant son, and work with my wife to figure out our schedules since she had a full-time job as well—all in the midst of a global pandemic. I thought it would be impossible to fit anything else amid all this madness.

That night, after I had the conversation with Monique, I thought to myself, *If I preach about having a mindset change, and believing anything is possible, how come I am not emulating the same attitude and conviction?* The very next day, I joined the writing group, and I knew I could figure things out as I went through the writing process. This is precisely what happened, I wrote close to 1,500–2,000 words every day and was able to write the majority of my content in 30 days. What pushed me to write every day, while balancing my family? The chance to impact people and change their lives. If this book is able to help you find your dream job, be successful, set you miles apart from the competition, and give you, your family, and others a better life, then I have accomplished my goal. Some people may ask, "Why did you have to write everything within a month?" I feel that this book is needed now more than ever before, and I needed to get it out into the hands of people, so they can transform their lives as soon as possible.

As for the book's theme: based on coaching numerous leaders in the industry and mentoring people in their careers, I realized there was a lack of resources and support to help people advance in their careers. There were no impactful tools available to guide individuals into the realization that they can always get their dream job and be successful. I started by reading quite a few career-related books. I felt none of them did justice in terms of weaving real-life experiences with practical strategies that could be immediately implemented in one's career. So, I decided sharing my strategies with the outside world was the right way to fill this gap and would help millions of other people who feel stuck, dissatisfied, anxious, and unfulfilled in their jobs. My memoir would have to wait (maybe it will be my next book. Hint, hint!)

I spent the first twenty years of my life thinking I was not good enough, I did not matter, I was dumb and stupid, and I let society give me a false identity. But after years of learning and research, I realized it was not true, and I can do anything I set my mind to. Society is going to tell you "do this thing," "do that thing," "this is what you are capable of," and much more. Don't let that form your identity. You know what is best for you. It is tangled within your mind. You have to unravel it gradually to find your own identity.

Your transformational journey starts with having focus, vision, goals, and purpose in life. For me personally, it was a gradual step-by-step process; it did not happen in a single day like in the movies. I was patient, I put in the effort, and I transformed my life from a shy, introverted kid to a successful, extroverted entrepreneur. It is never too late to make a change. I am an average person, and if I can do it, so can you.

Also, remember to always serve people. When you see how your work impacts other people and helps them lead better lives, that is when you get true joy and satisfaction in your job. Money and fame may be byproducts of this, but they should not be the end goal; your true intent will show through in your work, and if your motive lacks depth, so will your work. Reframe your mind to serve and lead.

I hope this book inspired you and made you realize that change starts within you. You are a badass, you have a gift, you are enough, and you can conquer the world.

So what are you going to do *next*?

Be Grateful, Stay Inspired
—Raj

Acknowledgments

There is a Chinese proverb which states, "A journey of a thousand miles begins with a single step." Each step of writing this book is attributed to the support of the many people who made this book a reality.

First of all, I want to thank my wife Carlene Subrameyer, who believed from day one when we first met that I could impact people's lives. It is her constant support that has made me accomplish incredible things in the past ten years. She is not only an ardent supporter of my work but also the initial design consultant and editor of this book, who gave me the first round of feedback. So, thank you, dear. Of course, I will be lying if I did not acknowledge the support and inspiration of our infant son, who provided me with immense support while writing this book. He kept cheering me on saying "bababa," which really brought a smile to my face and kept me motivated. Neil, I hope you will be proud of your Dad, especially the first time you read this book. I love you, son. I also would like to thank my Mom and Dad, who were nervous but supportive when I told them my plans of writing a book.

Secondly, I am grateful for Gahmya Drummond-Bey, my writing coach; Monique Lindner; and the entire writing group who supported me throughout my writing journey and made me accountable for my actions. Another person who was equally influential and helpful in guiding me through this process was my dear friend Mike Lyles, a published author of a great leadership book. He was able to guide me through the entire process of writing and publishing and even went out of his way to share all his secrets and strategies to success. Thank you so much, Mike. You are a great mentor and guide.

Writing is just one part of releasing a great book. There is design, editing, and the publishing process. I want to thank my friend and editor, Kelsey Kaustinen, who reviewed my drafts and provided great feedback to make the book more impactful. I thank my publishing company, who helped me get this book out to the world through various channels to impact more people.

Finally, I am grateful to my friends, and the entire community who follow my work. Your words, encouragement, and support pushed me to write this book in the first place. You showed me that what I do can impact people's lives, and this book is my way of saying, "Thank you!!!"